Master Home Music Production with Pro Techniques

Amir .M Escobar

All rights reserved.

Copyright © 2024 Amir .M Escobar

Master Home Music Production with Pro Techniques : Unlock Your Music Production Potential with Pro-Level Home Studio Techniques.

<u>Funny helpful tips:</u>

Stay updated with tax regulations; compliance is crucial for business longevity.

Stay reflective; learning from the past provides insights for the future.

Life advices:

Invest in digital marketing; online visibility drives sales in today's market.

Cultivate a savings habit; financial security provides peace of mind.

Introduction

Welcome to this book, the ultimate guide to help you kickstart your journey into the world of music production and recording from the comfort of your own space.

Discover the magic of Analog to Digital Converters and understand their vital role in the recording process. We'll unravel the mysteries of audio compression and limiting, guiding you through the controls and settings that shape your sound.

Are audio engineering schools worth it? We'll address this question and explore the power of practice and dedication in honing your skills. Learn about audio headroom techniques, ensuring your mix stays clear and professional.

In our home recording studio setup section, we'll recommend value-for-money gear to get you started on your musical adventure. From choosing the best computer and audio interface to finding the perfect microphone and MIDI keyboard, we've got you covered.

Mastering a song at home can be controversial, but we'll equip you with insights and methods to achieve exceptional results. Learn how to promote your music effectively on YouTube and attract real, targeted views and subscribers.

When it comes to recording on Cubase, we provide an A to Z guide, including recording WAV audio tracks, using the metronome, and mastering the art of MIDI recording.

Perfect your vocal mixing skills with our step-by-step guide on EQ, compression, and vocal effects. Find the ideal monitors for mixing and mastering, and delve into the world of reverb to add depth and richness to your recordings.

Understand VST instruments and explore the functionality of a Digital Audio Workstation (DAW). Unveil the purpose of an audio interface and its significance in the recording process.

With this book, you'll unlock the secrets of music production and step confidently into the realm of home recording, creating your unique sound and sharing your passion with the world. Let's start your musical journey today!

Contents

1. Analog To Digital Converter Tutorial – [AD/DAConverter] – The Reason It's So Important 1
What Does An Audio Converter Do 1
The Importance Of The Analog To Digital Converter 1
Cheap Converters = Bad Audio? 2
2. Audio Compressor and Limiting Tutorial – WhatIs Compression In Music Production? 4
An Audio Compressor Is Not So Complicated AsIt Seems 4
What Compression Is… In Simple Words 4
Knobs, Controls and Settings 5
How Do We Use A Compressor 8
Limiters VS Compressors 11
Limiters With A… Maximizer Role 13
A Second and… "Alternative" Use OfCompression 13
The Reason There Are Many Compressors 14
Conclusion 16
3. Audio Engineering Schools: Are they worth it? 17
Many people send me an e-mail asking me: 17
You Do Not Need A Degree To Do This For ALiving 17
Audio Engineering Schools Are Hyped 18
If you can pay for school, go! 19
Question: "Have you gone to an audio engineering school?" 20
What Really Counts 21
Practice… Practice… Practice 22
Nobody Can Stop You 23

4. Audio Headroom – How To Create More In Your Mix 25
Audio Headroom Techniques 25
Reduce The Volume Of Your Tracks 25
Stop Recording Too Hot 26
Beware Of The Low End 27
Use High Pass Filters 27
Compress The Low End 28
Low Mids Matter 28
Remove The Unnecessary Frequencies 28
Conclusion 30
5. Audio Latency – How To Optimize Your Audio Interface By Tweaking Your Buffer Size 31
The Reason The Default Sound Card Is Not Suitable For Music Production 31
What Is Audio Latency? 31
Tweaking The Audio Buffer Size 32
Important: 32
What Buffer Size Should I Choose For My Computer? 33
An Extra Mini Tip 34
6. Condenser VS Dynamic Microphones – Differences 36
Condenser Microphones 36
Large Diaphragm Microphones 37
Small Diaphragm Microphones 37
Dynamic Microphones 38
Large Diaphragm & Dynamic Mics 39
Condenser VS Dynamic Microphones 40
Final Words 41
7. Frequency Chart – The Most Important Audio Frequency Ranges 42

The Frequency Chart 42
0 – 60Hz (Sub-Bass) 43
60Hz – 250Hz (Bass or Main Bass) 43
120Hz – 350Hz – "Really Heavy Area" 45
250Hz – 2Khz (Low Mids) 45
2KHz – 8Khz (High Mids) 45
8Khz – 20Khz 46
8.   Gain Staging – How To Do It The Proper Way 47
Gain Staging Explanation 47
Noise To Signal Ratio 48
Clipping 50
How To Maintain Proper Gain Staging No Matter What 51
1)   Setting up the recording levels 51
2)   Maintaining our levels during mixing 52
Headroom 53
9.   Home Recording Studio Setup For Beginners –The Best 7 Value For Money Gear 54
Here's what you need: 55
Home Recording Studio Setup Essentials 61
Choosing The Best Computer For Home Recording 61
PC or Mac? 64
Best Audio Interface Under 200 Dollars 65
Reasons: 67
Best Studio Monitors Under 300 Dollars 68
How To Choose Studio Monitors 68
Best Headphones For Mixing And Mastering 71
Best Daw For Beginners 75

How To Choose Your DAW 76
Final Opinions – What Should I Get? 79
Best Microphone For Home Studio Setup 80
Best Midi Keyboard For Beginners 83
How To Choose A MIDI Keyboard 84
Best Value For Money Ratio Midi Keyboard For Beginners........................85
Conclusion 86
10.   How To Master A Song At Home – Mastering Is Hyped [Controversial] 89
What Is Mastering? 89
Mastering is Hyped 90
The Real Problem 94
There Are Mainly 2 Groups of Mastering Engineers 96
The 2nd Group 98
The One And Only Benefit of Hiring A Mastering Engineer 100
How To Master A Song At Home 102
Final Verdict 103
11.   How To Promote Your Music on YouTube Effectively 105
How To Get Real & Targeted YouTube Views and Subscribers – 105
Introduction 105
1.   Target Your Audience 106
2.   Create A Free Account 108
3.   Connect Your YouTube Account(s) 109
4.   Set Up Your Campaigns 111
4.b. Messages 114
You can easily change this, it does not have to be the exact same message but please pay attention to some critical points: 115
Here's the full and final message including the synonyms: 116

5. Explaining The Differences Of EachCampaign..117
Proof...118
I set up my campaigns and these are some of the comments I've got from people: .119
Talking about ranking…..123
But you know what? I got ranked on 1st Page!..124
And for the above reason, I ranked for a keyword that I would be thrilled to be on page 1. Check this out: 125
To Sum Up – We're Talking About: 126
12. How To Record On Cubase – The A to Z Guide 128
1.   Configure Your Audio Interface 128
2.   Configure Your VSTs 130
3.   Create New Project..133
Recording WAV Audio Tracks 137
Stereo VS Mono Track 138
Create Mono Audio Tracks..140
5.   Play With Metronome 149
Enable The Metronome 149
6.   Record MIDI 151
Recording Midi – The Steps 152
MIDI Track VS Instrument Track 154
The Difference Between the MIDI Track and the Instrument Track 154
Let's See How To Setup A VSTi Program Using The Instrument Track 156
It's easier than it seems..157
13.   Midi Tutorial – For What Midi is Used For 166
Midi Tutorial – A simple explanation 166
Is it necessary to own a MIDI Piano? 168
Converting MIDI to WAV..169

14. Mixing Vocals – How To EQ Vocals, Compress Them And Use Effects 170
Mixing Vocals – How To NOT Compress Vocals 170
Compressing Vocals Properly 176
Get Vocals To Sit In The Mix 176
The Difference Between Compressing Too Much and Compressing Wrong 177
My Vocal Plugin Chain 181
The Vocal "Warmer" 182
Vocal EQ Tips 184
Vocal Compression Settings and Tips 187
I Don't Have These Compressors – What To Do? 190
Vocal De-essing Tips 191

15. Monitors for Mixing and Mastering – Which should I choose? 193
The most important thing for us is to own monitors that they don't give a unique "color" to the sound. 193
High Budget Monitors 194
Update 195
What to look for in Monitors for Mixing and Mastering 195
Monitors with a Perfect Price to Value Ratio 197
Neither Expensive Nor Cheap Solutions 200
CRITICAL UPDATE – Winners in 2015 202
Conclusion 203

16. Reverb Tutorial – What Is Reverb In Music, What It Does, When We Need It And Its Controls 205
What Is Reverb In Music Production? 205
If We Could Give A Terminology For Reverb… 205
Why We Need Reverb 206
To Better Understand Reverb Let Me Give You An Example 206

Controls and Parameters – Reverb Tutorial 208
Room Types..210
Room 210
Hall 211
Plate 212
Spring Reverb 214
Clean Unwanted Frequencies Using EQ… EvenOn Reverb! 214
How Much Reverb Should I Use? What ReverbShould I Choose? 215
But I Would Not Like To Leave You Disappointed, So Here Are Some Quick Tips That I Can Share With You: 216
17. VST Instruments, VSTs and DAWExplanations 217
DAW stands for Digital Audio Workstation 217
VST stands for Virtual Studio Technology 218
VST Instruments...218
18. What An Audio Interface Is Used For –Definition 219
Definition 220
What Is An Audio Interface Used For..220

1. Analog To Digital Converter Tutorial – [AD/DA Converter] – The Reason It's So Important

Many people don't really know the importance of the audio Analog to Digital converter.

An AD/DA converter is converting the analog audio signal to digital. But why is this conversion necessary?

Let me explain.

What Does An Audio Converter Do

Our computer "lives" in a digital world with 0 and 1 commands.

When we record audio – an electric guitar for example – we transfer the sound from the real world (or analog if you wish) to our audio interface.

Our audio interface now needs to send the signal to our computer's CPU but our computer won't understand this signal since it's analog.

For this reason our audio interface has a built-in ad/da converter that handles the conversion. They "translate" the audio signal from analog to digital so our PC/MAC can recognize it.

The Importance Of The Analog To Digital Converter

If you've ever asked yourself the reason why a sound card that has only 1 Input costs hundreds of dollars more than a sound card that has multiple inputs, then these are the reasons:

It has less Latency.

They've got better Audio Converters.

While this conversion takes place the audio signal may get altered depending on the quality of the converter. The better the converter the better the final outcome that you'll hear coming out of your speakers.

Cheap Converters = Bad Audio?

Living in 2013, the technology that an analog to digital converter has is really superb.

While you can hear a difference comparing a sound card with a $1.000 converter to a $150 converter, that doesn't mean that the audio will suck. **No, it won't** .

Nowadays, even the cheapest converters will do the job without a single problem.

As I always say, the person behind the mixing console is the one that makes the difference and not the gear that the mixing engineer owns.

Why would you need to buy expensive equipment if you won't know how to use it? Firstly, spend some time improving yourself and then improve your gear. Happy mixing!

2. Audio Compressor and Limiting Tutorial – What Is Compression In Music Production?

Welcome to our new audio compressor tutorial that will show you how you can compress correctly including compression in series, limiting and coloring the sound using analog style compressors.

An Audio Compressor Is Not So Complicated As It Seems

Audio Compression create a sense of "fear" to people that just start their music production journey. The most familiar questions that people ask are "what is compression, **why** do we need it and **when** should we use it".

Truth is that if someone explains it **with simple words** then everybody will understand its use. And if you understand clearly **what compression does** then it's really easy to use it.

What Compression Is... In Simple Words

Think of a singer in front of his mic singing.

It's impossible for him to sing at a constant level during the whole song, there will be times that he will sing a bit louder and times that will go closer or a bit further from the mic, which is perfectly logical to happen cause no human can sing at the same exact level during the song.

It's also almost the same thing for everything. For example:

The bass player will hit the bass string a bit stronger and the drummer will hit the kick/snare/cymbal a bit stronger comparing to the other hit. **This makes perfect sense cause they are humans.**

Think of a Rock song – or Trance or Rap – imagine this song playing and its volume to constantly change or the singer's voice to be heard **sometimes louder and some times quieter in the same song** …

Wouldn't this be terrible? For this exact reason people have created the compressors!

To reduce volume if it exceeds a particular level of your choice, even if the singer sings louder at some point of the song, or the bassist hits the string noticeably louder or anything…

You can think of compression as a man standing in front of the volume faders/console and reducing the volume only to the louder parts of a song so that we can have a more "constant" volume throughout the whole song.

That's the main role of a compressor… We can also say that:

Compression is the procedure that we compress the audio signal in order to reduce the louder song parts and "match" them with the softer parts and achieve a more "constant" volume throughout the whole song.

Knobs, Controls and Settings

Like we said before, when the volume surpasses a particular volume level then the compressor starts compressing/reducing it in order to match it with the volume of the other parts.

But which is this **particular** volume level we're talking about and how do you configure it?

Well, you are the one that controls **how much** decibels the compressor will reduce, **how fast** it should cut them, **when** the compressor should start working… Everything can be configured by you and we'll see how right now:

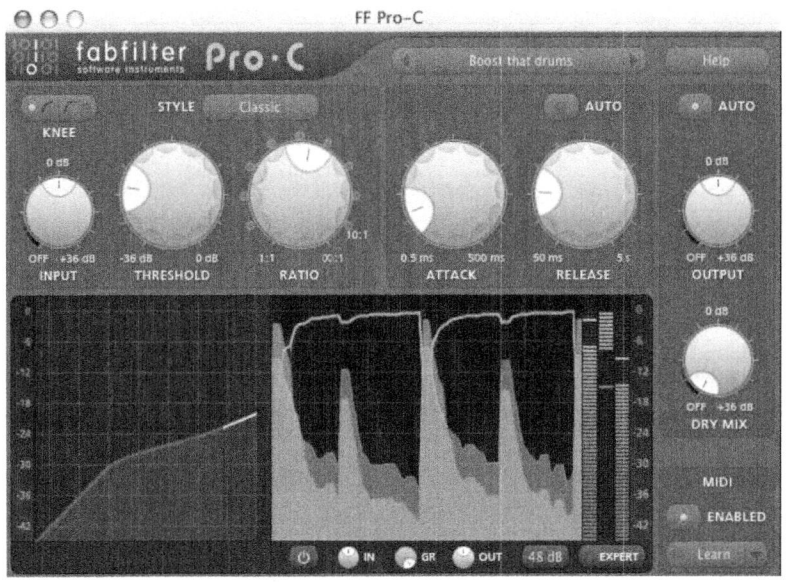

Threshold – How loud the signal should be in order for the compressor to start working. If the volume doesn't touch or surpass the Threshold then we will have no compression at all.

Ratio – How much compression we use. For example, if the Compression Ratio is set at 6:1, then from the 60db that surpass the Threshold we keep only the 10db. If we set the ratio at 2:1 we'll only keep 10db out of the 20db that will surpass the threshold and so on…

Attack – How fast – in milliseconds – the compressor "catches the signal" that surpasses the Threshold. 30ms Attack means that it will wait 30 Milliseconds and then it will "catch" the signal and start compressing it.

Release – How fast – in milliseconds – the compressor will release the signal after it compresses it and drop it back out of the Threshold. Most of the times the Auto function works properly.

Knee – It's similar to Attack but *not so important* that's why you may not see it on every compressor. Hard Knee means that our compressor will catch the signal aggressively and Soft Knee means that the compressor will catch it smoother and get "angrier" the further-er it surpasses the Threshold.

Make-Up Gain – When we use compression we reduce the signal so we need to get it back to where it was. If we compress 2db then we need to add 2db back.

Gain Reduction (GR) – This is how much db we reduce – Our main aim. Most of the times I find myself using up to -6db. Use more of this and the audio will sound "squashed" and definitely edited and we don't want the listener to think "something weird is going on here". If the listener that has no knowledge about recording and music production thinks that something is going on then we definitely didn't do a good job.

Output – You can increase or reduce the final volume. But since the compressor's job is not to increase the overall volume it's pretty useless for me. We have *Volume Maximizers* for that (which we will talk about in a different article).

Knee is not so important so you may not find it on every compressor.

Spend time practicing using the Threshold, Ratio and the Attack and the rest settings will be easier to configure.

How Do We Use A Compressor

1. No matter if you use an analog compressor or a VST compressor the setup is almost the same. Open your favorite compressor as an **insert** on the track that needs a compressor (mono, stereo, bus, group)

2. Adjust the Threshold so that the **Peaks (sudden volume changes or "spikes" that need to be reduced)** will surpass the Threshold narrowly. Unless you want to compress instruments that there's no problem if the compressor

compresses continuously, for example the bass guitar that can accept a sh*tload of compression cause it needs to be stable throughout the song.

3. Make the **Ratio** and the **Threshold** work together. Ratio is purely configured depending on the sound source but here's some nice starting points:

Bass – 4:1 to 8:1, Drums Group: 2:1, Vocals: 2:1 έως 4;1, Electric Guitars: 2:1 έως 6:1

Please treat the above information as **starting points** don't follow them blindly, take the initiative to experiment cause each sound is different.

4. Adjust the **Attack** and **Release** buttons, following the guidelines that I gave you above.

If your compressor has an **Auto** function on your Release button, then use it cause 80% of the situations it's gonna work right.

Too fast **Attack** will reduce the dynamics and kill the "feeling" of the song. Let me explain…
If in a specific part of a song the drummer **must** hit the snare **harder only at this spot** – cause the song demands it (it sounds better and make the listener go "whoa!") – then cutting this "attack" of the snare with too much fast compressor attack is not the best thing you can do.

But if you mix sounds with crazy **peaks** (sudden volume changes of the volume level) then you can easily chop off these peaks with really fast attack, even if it's only 1ms or 3ms.

I usually use fast attack on Mono Tracks with Instruments/Vocals with sudden peaks and slow attack on Group Tracks, where the compressor here plays the part of " I glue instruments together" rathen than "I work for a more stable volume between the louder and the quieter parts".

So as I always say… Keep your ears open and hear the changes that you make!

5. Use the **Make-Up Gain** to get the volume level back to where it was. The compressor's role is not to give volume.

But it is to give back the volume that the compressor reduced so that when we bypass the signal we hear the before and after sound with the same volume level.

If you have for example 6db Gain Reduction then you need to add 6db Make-Up Gain.

6. **You're ready!** Take a break and listen again. Make sure the volume levels between the sound with and without the compression to be the same. Why?

You may have compressed the signal in an awful way but your ears would think that you did a nice job because of the louder volume. Our ears always think that louder is better.

So for this reason, keep the volume the same NO MATTER IF THE COMPRESSOR IS ENABLED OR DISABLED. THAT'S VALID FOR EVERY TOOL NOT ONLY FOR COMPRESSION.

Limiters VS Compressors

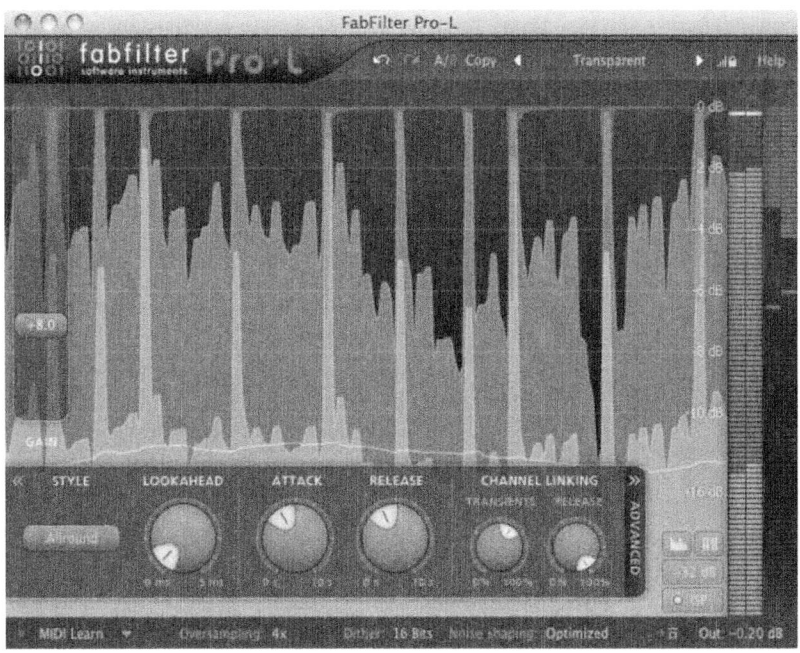

I'll create a different tutorial for Limiters but I would like to explain to you their basic difference with the Compressors. When the Ratio of the Compressor **exceeds 10:1** (meaning that it aggressively "chops off" the sound and doesn't "forgive" the decibels that surpass the Threshold) then we can say that the Compressor plays the role of a Limiter.

A Limiter is nothing more of a Compressor with a really strict Compression Ratio. Whatever audio signal surpassing the Threshold it gets chopped off aggressively so we must keep an eye on our Gain Reduction.

There's no written rule but you should aim not to exceed 3db Gain Reduction on a Limiter. The Limiter's role is to cut the sudden peaks and not to apply a smooth compression.

Limiters With A... Maximizer Role

Many Limiters, like Fabfilter L in the above photo, can also play the role of a Maximizer. They are **hybrids**.

Normal Limiters have a Threshold. You compress the signal to create stable dynamics and then you can dial back the volume using the Make Up Gain.

The hybrids though work the other way around:

The threshold is locked at 0db. You use the gain knob and give volume to the signal. When you reach and exceed the threshold then you apply limiting.

This way… you also **make the volume louder** plus you apply limiting to the peaks. 2 birds with 1 stone!

These kind of Limiters/Maximizers hybrids are perfect during mastering. You increase the final volume of the whole song and also cut the remaining peaks that would may bother the listener.

That doesn't mean that we can't use Limiters on **Mono Tracks** though.

If you have a Mono Track with a vocal/instrument that was recorded so bad and no compressor can fix the peaks then you can easily choose a limiter to do the job!

A Second and... "Alternative" Use Of Compression

As we said, the main purpose of a compressor is to match the higher volume levels with the lower ones.

But music and sound is art. So if we can create a new sound or modify the existing sound using the compressor... Why not do it?

Music producers like to experiment and use **lots of Gain Reduction with ultra high ratio (sometimes up to 30:1)** just so that they can "squash" the signal and push the compressors to the maximum.

This "overuse" of the compressor forces it to add a characteristic sound to the audio signal. While the "rules" say **do not over-compress**, sometimes by experimenting you can achieve some wonderful sounds.

What I like to do when I want to experiment – but also want to make sure that I don't destroy the sound by over compressing it – is to duplicate a track of mine and use all the crazy effects that I want on the 2nd track.

Then I blend the 2 signals together by adjusting the volume faders.

The Reason There Are Many Compressors

If you've ever wondered why there are many compressors out there since they do the same job then this is the answer: **Some compressors have their own unique sound**.

Also, some analog compressors don't have every single knob that I showed you above. Companies create them their own way, with only the most important knobs (Ratio, Threshold, Release, Attack).

That's the reason you come across thousands of topics on the internet "discussing" which compressor is better for vocals or guitars or bass…

From time to time you will end up creating your own favorite compressor list, no matter if it's analog or a digital VST.

Conclusion

I hope this tutorial to have answered all your questions about the basics of a compressor! If not please don't hesitate to leave a comment, positive or negative.

I don't know the exact money a teacher or a music school would ask you to give you this kind of information but I hope that this article will make you start practicing and improving yourself.

If you'd like to thank me consider sharing this post below or/and leave a comment, I am happy to see that this tutorial helps people, it motivates me creating more material for you guys.

☺
Happy mixing and happy practicing!

3. Audio Engineering Schools: Are they worth it?

Hello there, guys, on this post I am going to share with you my personal opinion about **audio engineering schools** and if they're worth it.

Many people send me an e-mail asking me:

1. Are Audio Engineering Schools worth it?

2. Will the school make you a better producer?

3. Is the degree worth in general?

4. Can I make money by mixing other people's albums?

You Do Not Need A Degree To Do This For A Living

I will answer you directly. You do not need any degree to record, mix or create full produced albums for artists.

Actually some of the most famous music producers have never gone to an audio engineering school.

Audio Engineering Schools Are Hyped

Let's say you're a customer looking for someone to record your mixes and your albums.

The No1 producer has a perfect production, a fantastic sound that will make you think "omg that's a fantastic sound" and the second one's sound is average.

Who would you trust?

The No1 producer of course. And what does this indicate?
That it does not matter if someone has a "better degree" than another's, cause his " degree" is his sound. There is no better degree and better proof that he knows what he's doing than his own sound that he can produce by himself.

Is this not reasonable? If the result is what you are looking for… Will you trust someone just because he has a piece of paper that says that "he is good, trust him"?

If I, as an artist, want a great sound for my album … then I'll pay attention that the sound he can produce is great for my album – simple as that – And not that he just owns a piece of paper.

If you can pay for school, go!

Before you think I'm against the audio engineering schools… Let me share my honest opinion with you… It's worth it only in some areas. For example …
* Public relations.
* Communication with other producers.
* You share your passion for music and sound.
* You can come in contact with high-tech recording and mixing equipment. All these concepts differ from school to school though. Unfortunately several schools, are not updated with the latest equipment and they are only worth for their "paper" (degree).

Question: "Have you gone to an audio engineering school?"

For some reason, many people ask me if I have attended to one of the audio engineering schools out there.

Reasonably, many people want to know if what I say is worth it – which I find perfectly logical – but I cannot reveal many details for obvious reasons.

Some people might think that I am getting paid for an "ad school promotion" and some people might think that going to school really matters…. For these 2 basic reasons I am not gonna say much.

But what I can say though is that I have went to school yeah. Was it worth it? Yes, but only for the things that I've mentioned above.

Could you live without it, if the pointers above wouldn't really matter for you? **Absolutely yes.**

There are countless tutorials on the web that teach you the same stuff as schools do and allow me to add that… they might be even better than *some* of the schools out there.

What Really Counts

Whether you go to school or not, if you do not spend some time practicing and exercising your ears, you will not succeed much.

No audio engineering school will take you by the hand and tell you "come on dear why aren't you trying hard… you're paying us, you should practice!".

If you have passion about music production and you love it then trust me… nothing will feel hard to achieve. You just need to spend hours in your home studio, **no matter if you go to school or not** .
You will learn from your mistakes and become better day by day.

Practice... Practice... Practice

Before I even started attending lessons in school I had started my own studio.

Yes it was pretty small and amateur at first, but I focused on things that mattered – things that would really improve my sound.

Do not spend money on fader-controllers with "cool lights". I've actually spent money on things that improved my sound – converters for example.

I am not gonna lie – I prefer using a controller rather than clicking a mouse.

But when I've heard the sound that I got after that I had upgraded my converters, then the "Shift+Click" method for an accurate and smooth level balancing didn't seem bad at all.

The secret is to make good choices in the beginning. Choices that someone will prefer YOU for your sound and not the "lights" on your console. That's what I did and earned my first money.

Showing off is not a way to make money. But if you insist on showing off something… **Show off your sound**. That's what matters.

When I had got my first money, then I got better controllers and amplifiers and slowly I've built an entire studio.

And all that happened because I had worked hard, I became better and I spent countless hours in front of amplifiers, microphones, computers and VST plugins.

Nobody Can Stop You

If you think you are "doomed" because you have not enough money to go to an audio engineering school, then there's really no need to worry.

Having not the opportunity to go to an audio engineering school, does not mean you're doomed to not learn about things that you love… It will just need a little extra effort, that's all.

If you're still worried that your songs won't reach the commercial sounding level because audio engineering schools are expensive as *insert word here*, then I'll try to create as many and high-quality tutorials as possible, explaining every single thing I do during mixing and mastering.

And I will be here to help you by answering your questions and offering my free lessons and tutorials.

Back to Mixing!

4. Audio Headroom – How To Create More In Your Mix

Welcome, today we'll talk about audio headroom and how we can create more of it in our mixes. It's really easy to do and it can be accomplished with stock plugins too, so there's no need to use third party ones.

Before we dive in we must understand that headroom can be achieved *during recording and mixing*. The reason I say this, is because I see some people new to home recording reducing the volume of the master channel thinking that this creates headroom.

The reason my dear friends this is not right, is because if the signal got clipped somewhere along in the routing path, it will still be clipped because the master channel is the **last signal receiver.**

Just by turning it down does not mean it solves problems, cause the problem is not in the master channel itself, but in the earlier stages of your DAW, which are your mono tracks, groups and bus tracks.

Audio Headroom Techniques

Since we started talking about clipping first, then the first way of creating more headroom to your mix is to…

Reduce The Volume Of Your Tracks

In the digital world of home recording, when your signal touches 0db in the track **it's clipped.**

Clipping means that there's suddenly a huge amount of distortion to your audio. And no I am not talking about the musical and gentle distortion that adds harmonics and clarity.

On the other side, "analog clipping" is gentle and you can see lots of engineers to drive the signal hotter in their analog consoles, getting some nice saturation and adding upper harmonics to the sound, which also adds clarity.

This is not the right way to do that on our digital consoles though. We use analog console simulators instead. We can't produce the analog console saturation effect just by bringing up our faders.

So please try to **Shift & Click all your Mono and Stereo tracks** and just lower them before you start sending them into groups and bus tracks. This will make sure that you're dealing with headroom correctly right from the start.

Stop Recording Too Hot

To be 100% correct, in order to deal with headroom correctly *right from the start*, the solution is not only to lower our volumes of our solo tracks, but it's also to record properly, because recording is the first and foremost step we should take properly.

I see people trying to record at around -3db with the peaks at 0db. Truth is that the peaks are over 0db, but our recording program cuts everything that is going above 0. There's really no reason to be afraid of recording lower, since we're not dealing with analog noise.

Our digital consoles have 0 noise, they're not producing noise themselves, the only noise we may have is the noise generated by our external gear. So since this noise-to-clean-signal ratio is so low, don't try to record near 0db all the time!

I usually record at -10 allowing the loudest peaks to hit at -3db. If I'm using [compression while recording](#) I record at around -7 and I still never let my peaks surpass -3. Then, I just turn my tracks down.

This way I'm sure I have enough headroom to play with and all my signals are healthy!

Please head over to the proper [gain staging tutorial](#) that shows you exactly how to record without causing artifacts.

Beware Of The Low End

The low end can be really sneaky and can creep up through our mix without even us realizing it.

There are various ways to deal with the low end in order to get some headroom and here are the 2 most common ones:

Use High Pass Filters

Using high pass filters everywhere except on your low end instuments, which are usually the bass guitar, the kick drum, an acoustic guitar or a synth with low notes, really helps.

Not only we're gaining audio headroom this way but we're also separating the [audio frequencies for a cleaner mix](#).

Compress The Low End

Compressing only the low end of your tracks gives you a lot of headroom, makes your track sound better and reduces frequency overlapping.

In order to compress just the low end area you need a multiband compressor and target a specific frequency range, usually ranging from 0Hz up to 100Hz.

Low Mids Matter

The same tips apply for the low mids up to ~300hz.

Using multi-band compressors here too is a perfect way to gain headroom, make the low mids tighter, clean some mud and generally improve your sound as a whole.

This trick is used also by Andy Sneap one of the most well-known metal engineers and he's using this tip to the electric guitars, by targeting the 100Hz to 300hz area and compressing it to taste.

Remove The Unnecessary Frequencies

Before reaching for the top end eq boost, ask yourself: *Maybe the track sounds dull and muddy, because it wasn't recorded so well?*

There's nothing wrong to boost to emphasize the frequencies the mix is asking for, but make sure you remove the ones that have got nothing to offer, but provide only muddiness and take up audio headroom.

You will also find out that by cutting the "bad" frequencies first, you won't need to boost as you had first thought.

Let me explain with an example.

Let's say that you have boosted at 6db with a high shelf at 5Khz to get some brightness. By removing the lower frequencies you'll find out that the track got brighter **without any boost**.

This is because that when we're cutting a frequency range, we're emphasizing the others *simultaneously and vice- versa*.

So instead of this 6db boost, you might have ended up with a 3db cut and a 3db boost instead (numbers are random generated for this example). The track *still has the same brightness and also sounds more natural this way.*

Conclusion

These are the most used techniques to gain audio headroom without sacrificing the audio quality. I hope this post has solved your questions about audio headroom and how to get it.

If you've got questions to ask, leave a comment below or join our community!

5. Audio Latency – How To Optimize Your Audio Interface By Tweaking Your Buffer Size

Welcome to *Audio Latency – How To Optimize Your Audio Interface By Tweaking Your Buffer Size* guide. In this tutorial I will show you how to tweak your settings for the best PC or MAC perfomance.

The Reason The Default Sound Card Is Not Suitable For Music Production

The most important reasons that the default sound card – the one you get when you buy a pc – can't help you record and mix are:

1) It doesn't have the necessary inputs we need to connect our mics (XLR Inputs) or the cables that our guitars and bass guitars need (TRS Inputs).

2) They have too much latency.

What Is Audio Latency?

With simple words we can say that:

Latency is the delay that exists in the sound from the time that the sound "enters" our audio interface and our DAW *until the time that "gets out" of our speakers.*

For example, if we have 10ms latency and play the guitar then we will hear the guitar's sound in 10ms (milliseconds). As you realized, the less ms the better.

We can easily record if the latency is up to 10ms but if it exceeds that limit then our ears start to anticipate it and it's too hard to record on time using the metronome.

For this reason, when you want to choose an audio interface, don't only pay attention to the input quantity but also keep in mind the latency speed it offers you.

Tweaking The Audio Buffer Size

Buffers optimize our computer's audio playback with the help of the AD/DA Converters.

I don't want to confuse you with technical terms because you won't need any of this info unless you want to build your own sound card, so I'll keep it simple.

Buffers are measured in **samples**.

The most used samples are: **256 samples, 512 samples, 768 samples, 1024 samples** and **2048 samples**.

Important:

- The less the samples the less latency we have, but we need a strong pc cause we need more resources.

- The more the samples the more latency we have, but we free pc resources especially if our pc is not powerful enough.

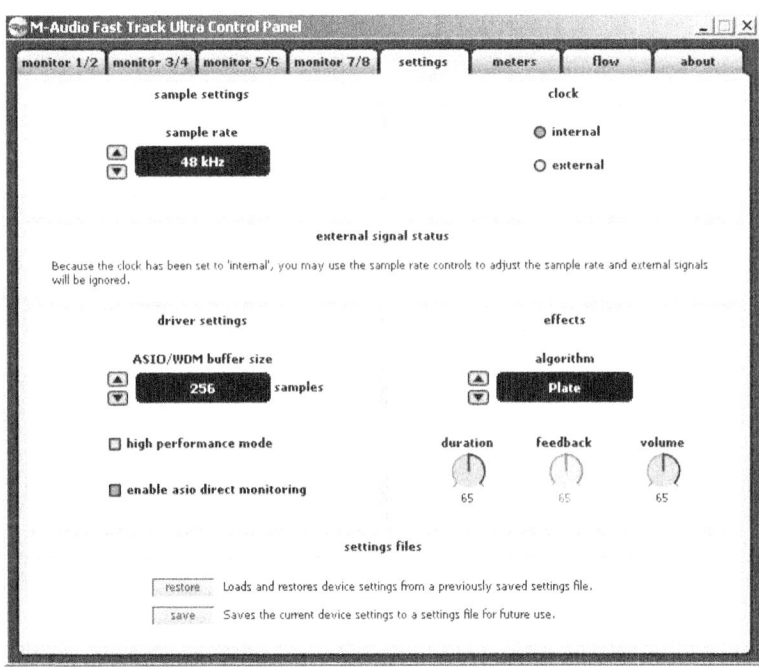

What Buffer Size Should I Choose For My Computer?

It really depends on the drivers of your sound card and your computer's processing power, but here's a sure-fire way to find the optimum buffer setings for your pc or mac:

1. Begin with the highest buffer setting (1024 buffers is a good start). The more you reduce them the latency will drop too.

2. You'll reach a point where your computer will start producing some strange noises during playback (also known as **glitches**). This is the setting that your computer cannot handle.

3. Raise the buffers to previous setting right before your computer started to produce these glitches.

I have an Focusrite Scarlett 2i2 at home and I have 8ms latency using 512 samples. Pretty cool if you ask me!

An Extra Mini Tip

Like we said above, less samples need more cpu power, so the more VSTs the more pressure we put to our computers.

To solve this problem we can record with the least samples possible (so that we can record with the lowest latency possible) and THEN raise the buffers when mixing.

Sound is not affected with this "method", we are done with our recording stage, so we don't really need to have low latency.

Let's "exchange" Latency with CPU power then for our mixing phase!

6. Condenser VS Dynamic Microphones – Differences

Welcome to the **Condenser VS Dynamic Microphones** post. Today we'll talk about these 2 huge microphone types and their main differences.

In the end of the post I will link you to my favorite microphone lists. For now let's see the benefits and drawbacks of each microphone type.

Condenser Microphones

Condenser mics are one of the most popular in recording studios. They are mainly used on instruments with *lots of dynamics* and *less volume – sudden transients* . Vocals (no metal brutals), acoustic guitars, violins and everything less transient oriented are mostly suited for condenser microphones.

Since they are *sensitive to louder sounds* you can rarely see them playing the main role on live shows. On the contrary, they produce a *wider frequency range* with better overall audio quality which is the main reason why they are used in silent recording studios, where audio quality plays a huge role.

This does not mean that dynamic microphones have less audio quality just because they produce less frequencies. Sometimes, depending on the situation (instrument) getting rid of some frequencies is *just what we're aiming for.*

Condenser microphones need some *extra power to work*, they need 48v more to operate. This is not even a problem since even the cheapest audio interface in the world can give you this kind of power. This switch can be found on the back of the mixer or on your audio interface.

In short, turn the switch on if you're using a condenser microphone and leave if off for dynamic microphones. Dynamic microphones don't need 48v of extra power.

Condenser mics tend to receive audio from *multiple directions* and not by 1 direction (front only) like dynamic microphones. So if your vocalist has the tendency to move while singing just let him enjoy it

Condenser mics are *usually* more expensive than dynamics ones. The word usually is important in this one. There are mainly 2 types of condenser mics.

Large Diaphragm Microphones

Large diaphragm microphones or LDMs are the ones that are mostly used on vocals. They tend to *warm up* the soun giving a richer low end and sweeter low mids.

They tend to change the recorded sound (in a good way) by *making it deeper and fuller*, since they tend to play with the low mids and the low end.

Small Diaphragm Microphones

Condenser mics with small diaphragms or SDMs are perfectly suited to reproduce a *frequency response that's more balanced with less to no warming effects*.

SDMs are also great at *capturing the dynamics with perfect detail*. If you want the most accurate representation of a wide and balanced frequency response including perfect dynamics, then the SDMs are the microphones to go.

Both LDMs and SDMs need a pop filter since they are sensitive to the Sss and Pop sounds. It's really hard to remove sibilance and popping during mixing so please try to record properly by using a pop filter and experimenting with mic positions.

Dynamic Microphones

Dynamic microphones can *withstand lots of transients and pressure* from hard hitting instruments. This is the reason they are mostly used on drum shells and on brutal metal and hip-hop vocals.

Dynamics mics are the ones that can be found mostly on live situations. They are not as sensitive as the condenser ones, moisture is not an abuse for them and they can withdraw lots of pressure.

As already mentioned above, they have a narrower frequency response but that's not necessary a bad thing, sometimes that's what we're aiming for.

Dynamic microphones receive audio mainly from 1 direction (front) so the singer should sing direct to it. This is perfect for home studio situations where the rooms – walls are not treated properly.

Last but also very important, dynamic microphones are *usually* cheaper than condenser ones. Cheaper does not always mean worse though.

Large Diaphragm & Dynamic Mics

Companies have started to listen to the wishes of home studio owners where soundproofing and proper room acoustics is an issue.

It's one of the reason companies are trying to create dynamic mics but with a larger frequency and dynamic response. I like to call these mics *hybrids*, but this is not an official term, just something I like to use.

One of these mics I personally use and love is the Shure SM7b.

Reasons? Its got most of the benefits of the dynamic *and* the diaphragm mics, at the same time. Plus, as a dynamic microphone it's cheaper than its condenser counterparts.

Many famous engineers call this mic their "secret weapon" and can be seen in lots of *behind the recording scenes* on famous albums, especially in rock and rap ones.

It works wonders on vocals, especially on aggressive like hip-hop and rock but also on non-aggressive vocals, guitar cabs, bass cabs and literally anything.

It's one of the dynamic mics that sounds like an expensive condenser microphone, but it's not as sensitive and as expensive as the condenser one.

In short: It's a steal. *The best price for value ratio* I've encountered in my whole audio engineering life.

Condenser VS Dynamic Microphones

While there's really no best than another I will recommend you the most suited type on which situation to use.

The only way to find what's best is to actually test it out on a music store, but if you googled your way here I suppose you'd like some free knowledge and *some shortcuts* to find the better ones, so there you go:

Vocals: LDMs are preferred. If money and proper room audio quality is an issue then go with a large diaphragm dynamic mic. If money is even a harder issue and you want to stay at the $100 range, then get the Shure SM58. Perfect for live *and* recording situations, also it includes a pop-filter on its own.

Drums: Dynamics for shells and a couple of condensers for Overheads and Room sounds.

Guitars on cabinet: Dynamics to withdraw all the cabinet air pressure. Especially the legendary and perfectly suited for guitar cabs Shure sm57.

Final Words

I won't go into too much detail about mic models cause this post talks about mic types. I'll make sure to create a new post about models and the reasons why I prefer a certain model over another. I'd like to keep the posts as nice and tidy as I can!

Feel free to subscribe to my newsletter on the right of your screen, leave a comment or follow me on twitter to be notified about the new post talking about mic models or anything else related to home recording and music production.

Thanks for reading and wish you the best! Have fun recording!

New post: Best Vocal Mic For Home Recording: Under $350.

7. Frequency Chart – The Most Important Audio Frequency Ranges

The "perfect" human ear can hear frequencies ranging from **20Hz** to **20.000Hz** (or 20KiloHz/Khz) according to the official frequency chart.

The average hearing range of the human ear though can hear from **50Hz** to **16Khz**.
The lower the Hz the bassier the sound. The higher the Hz the higher/brighter the sound. We can easily say that the more we grow old the less high frequencies we'll hear – usually from 18Khz to 15Khz – but we can hear the mids no matter our age.

The above are not a problem though cause music important frequencies can be found around 50Hz and 16Khz, so even if you are old and "lost" some frequencies don't worry, it's never too late to start mixing!

Also, [open a new tab to check out my latest lessons](#) and tutorials to improve your mixes!

The Frequency Chart

I broke down the frequencies into **6 main frequency ranges** .

This way it will be easier for you to practice and remember the frequencies. I am positive that this list will improve your mixing skills a lot.

Let's start!

0 – 60Hz (Sub-Bass)

0 – 35Hz: You can remove it completely. You won't find any musical information here. There's an "energy" that you can feel and will make your mixes sound dull and muddy, plus it will lose it's clarity. This kind of energy is really bad for your mix.

35 – 60Hz: You can still feel the energy rather than hearing it. Around **50** to **80Hz** you can find the wonderful energy that "hits you in the chest". This is the exact feel we have when we go to concerts and we feel the bass hitting our chest. It's an extremely important frequency range especially for Dubstep, Hip Hop, Drum & Bass etc... Since this sound is so sweet it's really easy to overdo it so please keep your ears open and mix correctly or you'll end up with the above drawbacks (muddy sound and no clarity).

60Hz – 250Hz (Bass or Main Bass)

The enhancement of these frequencies can make the sound "fuller" and "bigger". On the contrary, cutting these frequencies will make the sound "thin".

Depending on the sound, cutting these frequencies will also reduce the "muddiness". Every project/sound is recorded differently so you've also got to treat it differently.

60 – 120Hz: Fundamental frequencies for the kick bass and the bass guitar.

120Hz – 350Hz – "Really Heavy Area"

That's really the heaviest frequency area. Almost every single instrument has some frequencies in there.

Try to cut as many frequencies as possible from instruments that don't really benefit from these frequencies. And I don't mean to cut lots of dbs but just a couple of dbs would do the trick.

250Hz – 2Khz (Low Mids)

Here you'll find the fundamental frequencies of the most instruments.

By boosting these frequencies you'll make the sound fuller but if you overdo it you will cause ear fatigue to the listener.

The sound hurts the ear and you have a strange sense like "feeling the sound to your stomach".

2KHz – 8Khz (High Mids)

2 – 4Khz: Frequencies that help vocals and instruments to be more noticeable. You can achieve the same thing by cutting the same frequency range from different tracks than the one you're trying to make it more noticeable.

4 – 6Khz: Clarity. I should also mention that by boosting these frequencies the sound seems that it's closer you and by cutting them it seems to be afar.

8Khz – 20Khz

8 – 12Khz: Frequencies dominated by the cymbals.

8 – 16Khz: Clarity and sibilance. It's really important to record properly without "Sh's" in the vocals so can you boost for clarity in case you need it, without worrying about the sibilance.

12 – 20Khz: "Air". It gives the sense of air and openness in the mix.

8. Gain Staging – How To Do It The Proper Way

Gain staging is the one of the easiest and most crucial tasks in your home recording studio adventure. It takes only 2 seconds to implement properly and it's so easy that many people don't really care about it.

The results of not caring about gain staging can make our lives harder during mixing, so let's learn how to use gain staging properly (since it only takes 2 seconds to do it) and save ourselves time and effort.

Gain Staging Explanation

Gain staging is simply put the procedure of getting a healthy signal while recording into your DAW. But what do we really mean by healthy signal?

Assuming you've experimented with your microphones and mic positions in your home recording studio, you should record in a manner so that you can get as loud as it gets signal, taking into consideration the rules below.

If you're working with MIDI the same principles apply. The difference is that instead of tweaking your Gain Input Knob of your audio interface to set the recording levels, you will tweak the output signal of your VST instrument.

A healthy input signal with proper gain staging consists of:

No clipping.

Minimum signal to noise ratio.

Enough headroom to play with dynamics during mixing.

I would add that the source sound – *captured by a mic, sample or synth sound doesn't matter, all of these are considered source sounds* – should be as great as possible cause as we already know *good* sound in = good sound out. This isn't a post dedicated on sound design, so I'll leave it for a different post.

This is a post dedicated to **how to import our already greatly created sounding signal to our recording software without reducing its quality on its way in**. Assuming we have already created our sound (and it sounds great yeah!) now it's the time to import it with proper gain staging.

Let's start by explaining the noise to signal ratio.

Noise To Signal Ratio

When you record through a microphone you receive different volume stages of the signal. To better help you understand what I mean, I'll use as an example an electric guitar recorded through a $50 cabinet.

Crank the gain up to maximum. Can you hear the noise? There's a 99% chance you'll hear hiss noise with the gain cranked up to death on a $50 guitar amp-cab combo.

Now hit some strings.

How louder is the actual sound from the noise when you mute the strings? Is the volume of the noise close to the actual music? Then the ratio is small. You should minimize or remove noise.

Is the noise almost *not* there when you're playing? Then the ratio or difference in volume between the two is huge. Good job, proceed to recording or remove noise completely if you can and then hit the record button.

Why is this so important?

Because when you reach the mastering phase where you'll bring up the whole track's volume as a whole, if the volume difference between great sound and crappy noise is minimal, then noise will creep up to you and say "Hey! I sense a volume maximizer here. I'm in".

Clipping

Clipping is fairly easy to comprehend. Back in the day, when analog consoles were the only consoles available, engineers used to drive the signal nuts so that they could give harmonics and grit to the sound. Nowadays, people still do the same trick and works wonderfully.

If you try to go past 0 db on our recording software to get the same saturation effect, I assure you you're gonna punch your monitors for the sound they'll deliver to you. It's not going to work. Our digital consoles have a limit and we should never surpass it.

Does that mean that we, the digital users, can't get the same analog console saturation effect?

Of course we can! But we do it with VST plugins instead that emulate the analog console sound and not by just increasing the volume.

Here's how:

How To Maintain Proper Gain Staging No Matter What

Some people think that proper gain staging can be achieved only by setting the recording levels right. They're right but that's only half the battle.

We start by proper gain staging on our audio interfaces and then we should maintain it through our plugin chain too. Let me explain.

1) Setting up the recording levels

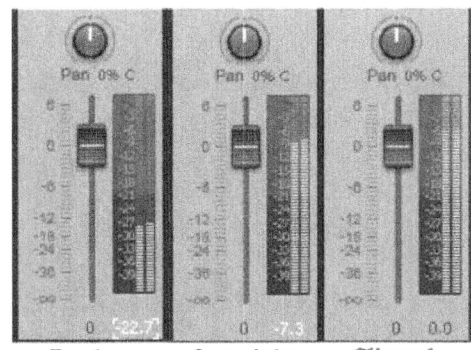
Too low   Just right   Clipped

In the image above you should notice something really important. The volume faders are the default stage. The volume is being tweaked by your **input knob on your sound card** or by the **output volume of your VST MIDI instrument**.

Assuming you created a great sound that you like, hit that record button and play with the gain knob to achieve the desired results.

I usually record at -10 allowing the loudest peaks to hit at -3db. If I'm using compression while recording I record at around -7 and I still never let my peaks surpass -3. Then, I just turn my tracks down in the mix if needed.

2) Maintaining our levels during mixing

How many times have we changed the actual volume of the track when we add a vst plugin? Lots of times!

I remember myself when I had first started 6 years ago, when I didn't have enough volume on the track, I was just increasing the volume using the output of a random plugin. *OK I'll hide in a cave for doing that...*

If you're also doing that, let me explain to you why there's really an output fader in each and every plugin. And it exists for 2 main reasons:
To prevent the plugins from clipping . Plugins clip the sound too if they add volume, a perfect example is the saturation type of plugins.

To have the exact same volume with and without the plugin . Our ears get tricked way too easily if the sound is louder.

The only way to really understand if the sound is *better* and not just *louder* is to *create the same volume between the bypass and active mode of the plugin*.

So if you're scratching your head trying to find where the clipped sound is coming from, look at one of your plugins! Also if you feel there's a volume difference when you're bypassing a plugin, fix the output of the plugin! It's critical to not forget that gain staging exists in our plugins too.

Headroom

I mentioned above that gain staging helps create headroom in your mix. It's true that proper gain staging can be achieved by setting the recording levels right, but that's only the 1st step to take care of.

Headroom can be achieved with multiple tricks and there are 6 – 7 major methods to get headroom without sacrificing the sound. In order to keep everything nice and tidy, visit the separate headroom post to learn about all the methods.

Hope I explained it to you as simple as possible. If you got any questions, please visit our forum and we'll help you in no time.

9. Home Recording Studio Setup For Beginners – The Best 7 Value For Money Gear

Welcome to *Home Recording Studio Setup For Beginners – The Essentials* , the A to Z guide that will help you build your own home studio in no time.

If you're a home recording enthusiast, you may have wandered the internet checking out recording studios and the first thing you might have noticed, is the huge rooms with the tons of hardware processors.

Here's what you need:

Click here for the checklist!

If you've seen all these processors and thought "damn it costs a fortune to build a studio" then I've got some great news for you. **You don't need to own anything that you've seen**.

A computer with an audio interface and some other minor stuff like cables are enough to get you going. Even famous producers and audio engineers are going full ITB (In The Box – meaning that they use only processors in the computer and not *out of the box* or out of the computers).

Technology is fantastic right? Famous analog processors with their unique vibe and sound that used to use the space of a whole room, can now be used inside our computer.

Can we achieve commercial sounding recordings with a home recording studio setup for beginners?

I used to use analog processors and expensive monitors, but life demanded I find lots of money in less than a year, so I was forced to sell anything expensive I had in my studio.

It hurt... **a lot**. Thankfully, my mixing and mastering experience could not leave me too, and in the end, *I am happy I was "forced" to mix and master with the lowest budget gear*.

What I found out is that I **achieved the exact same results.**

The engineer's experience behind the gear plays the most important role and not the gear itself. New producers, mixing and mastering engineers spend tons of money upgrading the gear because they think that's the reason their mixes can't touch the commercial sound.

I created this post to prove that the basic low-budget gear along with some VST plugins are more than enough for you to produce a commercial sounding track.

You may also notice a bit of strong confidence in my words. The reason is that I've spent more than 6 months actually buying and testing out everything in the *same price range*. I would never post something without proof, especially with that kind of confidence.

Reasons to trust this post.

This post was written in 3 days but this was not the real time needed to create a solid article with proof. You cannot buy a piece of audio gear and expect to know exactly how it works, including their flaws and benefits, in a day or two.

I needed to give at least 1 month to each piece of gear, before selling it and moving to the next one (in the same price range) and compare the two.

The 2nd reason that I am pretty confident about this specific setup is that I *am giving you live audio samples produced with this specific gear you're going to read below in this post* .

Check out this page of mine to listen to some tracks mixed and mastered by me with the gear you're going to see below: My Work – Audio Samples .

The audio samples that you listened to, were produced using only VST plugins and using the exact same home recording studio setup for beginners that you're going to read below.

If you felt like the audio wasn't up to your expectations, then ditch this guide completely. If you liked the audio I managed to produce out of this specific setup and you feel is decent for you and your home recording studio, then here's what I've got to say:

If I managed to create a sound (with the home recording studio beginner setup you see below) that you liked and you would like to achieve, then I just proved to you that spending money on new gear *is not the solution* to a commercial sounding recording. **Please help me save your money**.

If I made it with just a computer, some plugins and mixing speakers in the $290 range, what holds you back of doing the same? *Practice* is the answer. I am not smarter than you guys.

I just spent time practicing along with training my ears. Buying new gear all the time, without knowing why, won't improve your mixes at all.

If you've got a store near you that lets you hear some gear before buying then I advise you to go there and listen to the gear first. If you own something *similar* from the list below you don't need to go and buy the gear I recommend (as long as you're happy with yours of course).

No matter how much I truly love the gear I mention to this post, the only way to be 100% sure that you're going to love them as much as I do, is to actually hear them.

But since you searched for an online guide, I suppose you either don't have this kind of privilege near you or you just want to read some opinions.

Let's start with the necessary home recording beginner list, shall we?

Home Recording Studio Setup Essentials

I'll start with some bullets and then I'll explain and talk about each and every subject thoroughly, so you can get the best value for money ratio.

Important: **Just because something costs more does not mean it sounds better.** While this is true in general, it's even more true if we talk about audio gear.

So my aim in this post, is not only to show you how to build your own home recording studio, but also to **save you money** by pointing you to the right direction and gear.

Gear and [free mixing lessons](#) for you that will help you produce a track with commercial audio quality.

Choosing The Best Computer For Home Recording

Since you're a beginner in home recording, you should not worry about outboard compressors or EQs – even pros don't nowadays with all this brand new technology.

I am going full ITB (In The Box) in the moment and I don't miss my analog gear at all, but I'll stop here cause I don't want to transform this guide to a "Analog VS Digital" topic.

I am in love with modern recording – mixing techniques and sooner or later some of the analog fanatics will come and spread some inaccuracies and I want to get rid of that.

So, back to the point, here are the main parts of a home recording computer:

CPU RAM

Yes, that is all. If you've got money to invest for a great home recording computer that's the 2 main parts that you should invest most of your money in.

Plugins need processing power and RAM.

I've found out that CPU is mostly used on plugins like EQs, Compressors and Reverb analog-modeled units, while RAM is mostly used on libraries like Kontakt Libraries.

If you're composing hip-hop or orchestral music for example, then you will need lots of RAM in order for your computer to load every single velocity of each library.

More velocities = better, cause you can play with the velocities and make the audio sounds like it's played by a real human and not a computer.

No matter if you're using libraries or not, you're going to need lots of CPU for your compressors, delays, reverbs, EQs and saturation plugins.

There are some plugins that actually mimic the analog sound of its "real" analog counterpart, thus the need for processing power.

You can save money by getting a mediocre graphics card, so it's better to invest those dollars for a better CPU and RAM combo, as long as we speak about a home recording computer and not a gaming computer.

PC or Mac?

The reason I started by mentioning the necessary hardware components of a home recording computer, and not the Operating System, is because **the hardware is what really matters** .

People have been fighting for ages – and continue to fight – about which OS is better.

I believe the right question to ask is: *How well do my audio interface drivers work along with my Operating System?*

I owned a MAC for 3 years. Then I needed to upgrade my computer – since I wanted to go full In the Box – but I didn't want to spend a fortune to do it.

So I thought to give Windows a go. I installed Windows 7 with the Service Pack 1 and my audio interface's drivers. My preferred company for audio interfaces is RME, which is known for its solid drivers.

To tell you the truth, I noticed no difference between the 2 Operating Systems. People claim that Windows crash a lot, but I had absolutely no problems with a fresh install of Windows 7 and the latest driver's version of my audio
interface.

So I was happy that I went with Windows, cause I would need around $1.500 more to get the same CPU and RAM power on a MAC.

Final verdict? Focus on getting decent hardware and work with the OS you're used to and you'll be fine!

Best Audio Interface Under 200 Dollars

Now that we've made some things clear about computers it's time to get an audio interface.

But what's an audio interface?

An audio interface is simply put, your sound card. It's the device that communicates with your computer, converting the audio signal from digital to analog and vice-versa.

It's also the device that gives you the option to select how far you want to push your CPU power, by adjusting the buffer size. Lower buffer size = less recording latency but more CPU power is needed, while a higher buffer size does the exact opposite.

The most important factors to take into consideration, while choosing an audio interface though, is the number of inputs and outputs. No matter how many inputs an audio interface may have, you can record a full album using only one input.

Even professionals choose to record each instrument separately when recording a whole band. Drums usually go first. You really don't need to use all inputs at the same time, so we'll save lots of money by choosing an audio interface that's got just the necessary ones.

After lots of tests and in-depth search, I came to the conclusion – well not only me, but also the rest of the home recording world out there – that the best value for money audio interface is the Focusrite Scarlett 2i2.

Reasons:

Stable drivers – It's really hard for it to crash, both on Windows or Mac.

Direct Monitor – It's a pretty unique and fantastic feature of this sound card. When you record, you enable it and you get almost 0ms in latency. This is more important than you may think and other sound cards, in the same price range, while they have this feature is mostly found in the software. Having a knob for easier workflow is a plus.

Best value for money ratio – I've tried out similar audio interfaces to this price range (or even $50 more) and no other sound card was as good as this.

2 Inputs – While 1 input is enough for home recording projects, what if you want to record yourself and your guitar at the same time? With 2 inputs you can.

Best Studio Monitors Under 300 Dollars

The studio monitors I'm going to mention right now, can easily change the title from the *Best Studio Monitors Under 300 Dollars* to the *Best Studio Monitors Ever* ~~Under 300 Dollars~~.

See what I did there? With these speakers, some plugins and your mixing skills of course, you can easily achieve a commercial sounding track.

How To Choose Studio Monitors

I want to save you time, so instead of pointing out the reasons I went with the $300 monitors in this article, I've included everything here: Monitors for Mixing and Mastering – Which should I choose?.

I highly recommend you to check it out, it's got anything you need to know about monitors and I also included the reasons I preferred these particular ones.

While the article above has detailed information, I'd like to add the most important aspects when choosing monitors here:

The monitors must be true and not "lie" to you – They must not have exaggerated bass, mids or high end. They must be as *flat* as possible.

They must be clean and able to produce each and every frequency – You need these monitors to mix, thus you need quality and in-depth sound.

So back to the point... These are my beloved studio monitors:

The monitors above are the JBL LSR 305 Monitors.
These are the monitors I own right now and I cannot describe how happy I am that I decided to give them as shot. My mixes translate so well on every audio system I could not believe they actually cost less than $300. I felt like that
the company was stealing itself. I've got much respect for the developers, offering fantastic quality with the lowest price.

These guys even kick some serious "behind" between its famous competitors such as the KRK Rokit or the Yamaha 5 inch speakers.

You can also check out the Amazon Reviews: **4.9 out of 5 stars**. We should not rely solely on amazon reviews though, because as mentioned, we should always actually use something to create an impression. Amazon reviews and hundreds of home recording enthusiasts praising these monitors though, is a huge plus.

I've found an amazon deal that includes both of the monitors and cables, for just **$280 for everything – 2 monitors and cables**.

This deal is pretty sweet, so do yourself a favor and please don't order the monitors by piece, because (including the cables), the price would surpass $300.

Why spend more than 300 dollars when can you get everything for $280? Click the image below to get redirected to the deal (I hope it's still active):

I'd like to add something important: If your room is untreated and you feel like the bass is getting exaggerated by the reflections of your wall, then these monitors have a a couple of switches on the back. It's got 2 switches with 2 options each. You can boost or reduce 2db for the low end or/and the high end.

What I did was to use the low end switch, removing 2db of the low end and I left the high end switch at the default setting. You really don't have to do the same, each room is different, but having options like these is powerful, cause you can calibrate the monitors according to your own room sound.

This information is not to be replaced by proper room acoustics configuration, but let's be true here. We're talking about how to set up a home recording studio for beginners, if I were to tell you to spend thousands of dollars fixing your room acoustics, while trying to show you the best *value for money gear*, then this post would be a joke and lose its focus.

While having a proper sounding room helps, it's not mandatory for a *home* **recording studio.**
As long as you can reference your mixes to commercial tracks and mix according to your reference tracks, then nothing is stopping you to create a similar commercial sound.

If you really feel like that your room has way too much "reverb" in it that no monitors will work in there whatsoever, then consider reading the chapter below. A man mixed a number 1 record entirely on headphones, so it's achievable.

Best Headphones For Mixing And Mastering

This step is not necessary for your home recording studio setup. This is optional, but it's recommended to read this chapter for extra knowledge.

When trying to find the best headphones for mixing and mastering the same principles apply, just like when searching mixing speakers. The sound must be real and not exaggerated in highs, mids or bass. Headphones must sound as *flat* as possible. I've tried 5 headphones for mixing and mastering, 4 of them sucked, I could add them here but bashing is really not my cup of tea.
Instead of focusing on negative statements and on what you should avoid, I prefer to focus on *what really worked*. My own preference (and almost 80% of the rest home recording world out there) prefer to mix and master using the Sennheiser HD 600 headphones.

Will Putney [mixed a number 1 record entirely on these headphones](#) and explains the reasons he'd chosen these particular headphones.

Important Note: If you own monitors, then headphones are completely optional. There are some benefits depending on each situation though, like:

1. Respect your family or neighbors – If you primarily work at night then headphones can help you mix and

master while not bothering your family. This does not mean that you can't mix on monitors on low volume too. If the rooms are not next to each other then definitely go for monitors.

2. Not Enough Room – If you've got no room to put your monitors to, you can get headphones.

3. Use them as Reference – It's always wise to switch to a different playback device, to kind of "refresh" your ears, and then switch back to your monitors again.

It's always better to mix on monitors, your ears will last longer on each mixing session. The good thing about
the Sennheiser HD 600 headphones though, is that they don't have harsh high mids and you'll be able to mix for many more hours compared to other headphones.

Since this guide talks about the Home Recording Studio Setup Essentials, and one of my targets is to save you money, I recommend you to ditch headphones completely and practice mixing on speakers. If money is not an issue, then go for both.

A cheaper alternative: If the Sennheisers seem too high for your budget, consider getting the Sony MDR 7506 headphones. These are my 2 favorite headphones, I give the HD600s a 4.8/5 and the MDRs a 4/5. It's really hard to find better headphones in this price range, but if you do, leave a comment and I'll make sure to test them out and update the post!

Headphones for tracking vocals: If you plan on recording someone, then don't spend a fortune on headphones. The vocalist will be happy enough to wear headphones, he doesn't really cares about frequencies and stuff, as long as he can hear himself. Don't worry about getting expensive headphones for vocal tracking, let's save some money for now.

Best Daw For Beginners

Another important component for your home recording studio setup is to choose a DAW.

If you don't know what a DAW is or does, please check out this article. If you're bored to read the article, then a DAW is simply put the program you're using to record, mix and master.

The most popular Digital Audio Workstations are Cubase and Pro Tools. A couple of others are Ableton, Studio One and Reaper.

I can't really tell you which DAW is the best or which sounds best, because there's really no sound difference between the DAWs. Some people swear that they can hear slight differences, but let's not change the subject of this post. *[cough]* But all daws sound the same *[/cough]*.

I've used a total of 4 DAWs in my life, for at least 1 year per daw (I am a daw freak I know), so I hope my experience will help you decide which is best for you. Before I tell you which I'm using right now allow me to explain how to choose your own recording software.

How To Choose Your DAW

All DAWs do the same job and have been created with the same target in mind: To help you produce, record, mix and master music.

It really doesn't matter for the listener to know how you've created a song. He really doesn't care, all he cares is the sound of the song and the song itself. Think of yourself as an example…

When you listen to a song on youtube, do you really care if the producer used Pro Tools or Cubase? Nope. All that matters is the final product.

Choosing a recording software is similar to choosing a car. The final destination **(song)** can be reached quicker depending on how well you know how to drive your car **(shortcuts)**.

Knowing how to **take advantage of the shortcuts and the general flow of your software, then that's the best daw for you**.

But since you can't try out every single daw out there, let me help you with these statements:

Pro Tools – Mostly used for mixing and mastering purposes. Great routing workflow but lacks in MIDI.

Cubase – It has one of the most powerful MIDI editors. Especially useful for composers that use heavy kontakt libraries (cinematic, orchestral, hip-hop, etc).

Studio One – Similar workflow and shortcuts to cubase. It's like a modern version of cubase with some "fresh" minds developing it. Great MIDI workflow too.

Reaper – This has got a [downloadable demo version](#) that never expires. It's super simple, has got different workflow and shortcuts from Cubase and Studio One. A huge plus: It's got the most user-friendly community in the history of DAWs.

Ableton Live – Mostly used for EDM productions. Easy workflow and also has the ability to automate everything you click, thus the name

Live.

FL Studio – Mostly used for EDM productions.

I started off using Cubase, since my main aim was to compose cinematic music. Then I switched to Pro Tools, because I was really curious to know why so many people use it. I felt that the reason behind it was its great mixing workflow, but it was lacking in MIDI so I thought I'd try something else.

I downloaded Reaper. I fell in love with its simple, yet powerful workflow and tools. But I believe reaper would be awesome for those that haven't been used to Cubase like me… Reaper's shorcuts were really different from Cubase's ones, so I needed to find something similar to cubase.

I didn't want to go back to cubase cause I was tired with all the updates and, as mentioned, I am a DAW maniac. So, for the past year I've been using Studio One. I'm currently in love with it, it's got almost the same shortcuts like cubase's got and a drag and drop feature that I can't live without.

Cockos Reaper 4 Interface Overview

Final Opinions – What Should I Get?

The final verdict is to try as many as you can by downloading the demos, but my personal view is to go with *Reaper*, especially if you're a beginner and have never tried out something else.

It's so simple, yet so powerful you'll love it, plus its demo version never expires – but please support the developers if you like it, they're worth every cent.

If you've got more money to spend, then go for cubase or studio one. Both work in similar ways. Cubase's super benefit is its powerful MIDI editor while Studio One's powerful and unique feature is its *drag and drop* workflow. I went with Studio One.

If you're really indifferent about MIDI features, then go with Pro Tools.

They've been designed with the recording-mixing-mastering mindset, not really caring about MIDI. Be prepared to spend a fortune though. **Pro Tip:** Get reaper and save your money for beers. OK chill man, it's your money I won't tell you what to do, Jesus.

Best Microphone For Home Studio Setup

A vocal microphone is necessary for your home recording studio setup, as long as you plan to record others or yourself. If you're composing instrumental music then you can ditch the vocal microphone completely and purchase some kontakt libraries (pianos, violins, drum-kits, etc).

If you really want to record vocals then there's a home recording vocal package out there, that it's impossible to beat its value for money ratio. The package I'm talking about is the package in the image below:

Why is this considered to be the best microphone package for a home recording studio setup for beginners? Here are the reasons:

It was built with the home recording beginner studio in mind. It's got anything you need to record properly.

The microphone has top-notch quality audio. Great sound and noiseless. Free popshield.
Free shockmount. Free XLR Cable. 10 Year Warranty.
Rode NT1A – Studio Secrets. Tutorials and guides for getting the best sound out of your Rode NT1-A.

I know that many high-end gear fanatics will start bashing the post commenting that "there's no best mic, each mic is different", so in order to make this post as informative as possible, I've got to say that I partially agree with them. There really is no best microphone in the world, because each mic has its sound.

But the package I mentioned above is really the **Complete Vocal Recording Solution**, especially for someone who's just entering the home recording world. I speak from personal experience that this package is the real deal, I've also experimented with more expensive microphones, but the Rode Nt1 is a mic I find myself using it all the time.

Plus, for what you get, you really can't go wrong with a 10 Year Warranty for $229 from this amazon deal. I've spent $1.000 for a single microphone and sold it to get something that cost $300 and I was happier with it. Let us not judge audio quality by its price.

Best Midi Keyboard For Beginners

While you can use your computer keyboard to play notes, one of the drawbacks that I've found is that it lacks a **Modulation** control like in the image below.

The reason I find that I need a modulation control is when I use Violin Libraries.

I adjust the **modulation control to play the role of the velocity**. It's smoother and way more natural to record violins while playing with modulation to change its velocity.

On the other side, if you're producing music with almost no need of dynamics – such as rock, techno, EDM, hip-hop and rap – I strongly advise you **to save your money**. You can easily fix the dynamics using your mouse in the midi editor later.

To tell you the truth, we all know that hard style genres don't really need dynamics, instead we focus on getting an aggressive and in-your-face sound. Natural dynamics are crucial for orchestral music, but for hard genres we can live without the modulation control.

How To Choose A MIDI Keyboard

If you still feel the need that you want to buy a MIDI keyboard no matter what, then here are some pointers you should consider before purchasing. You should ask yourself: "What exactly changes the price of a MIDI keyboard?".

There are 4 huge factors that determine the price of a MIDI keyboard:

The quantity of keys.

The quality of the keys – Are the keys velocity sensitive? The extra controls such as a built-in mixer.

Transport controls.

Quantity of keys: You can find midi keyboards with 25, 49, 61, 76 and 88 keys. The more the keys the more money they will cost. 49 or 61 keys are enough for most people, while 76 and 88 keys seem a bit of an overkill. On th other side 25 keys are not really sufficient even for a home recording studio. I would go with 49 keys, unless I have more room on my desk where I would aim for 61 keys.

Quality of keys: Even the least expensive midi keyboard have velocity enabled keys. Plus, most keyboards have quality keys nowadays in the $100 price range. I would aim for no less than $100 when considering to get a midi keyboard with quality keys.

Extra Controls: Some midi keyboards have extra knobs, buttons and switches. You can configure them to work in conjunction with your recording software so you can be able to play with the faders without using a mouse. If money is an issue and my aim is to get the best value for money ratio I would ditch the extra controls completely.

Transport Controls: Living in 2015, even the cheapest midi keyboards have transport controls now. The midi keyboard I am going to suggest below has also got transport controls that work flawlessly with most recording programs and applications.

Best Value For Money Ratio Midi Keyboard For Beginners

One of the best keyboards that's got everything that you *really* need is the M-Audio Keystation 49.

It's got transport controls, great keys with velocity sensitivity, 49 keys which are more than enough for a home recording studio setup, modulation and pitch bend controls and only costs $99.

You really can't beat a price like that for a quality midi keyboard for your home recording studio setup, that also includes the fundamental controls for your music production needs.

Conclusion

There you have it. The gear mentioned above are the perfect essentials for a home recording studio setup for beginners. My aim was not only to satisfy the home recording beginners though. Someday you won't be a beginner anymore, so I had **one more target** while writing this post.

My second, yet important target I focused on, was to provide you with gear that won't need to be replaced in the near future. Practice will make you better in some months, your experience *will* improve, but everything I mentioned will stil work more than fine. You won't have to replace something if your experience improves.

A great example of this, is the monitors that I mentioned above. The more you use them the more you love them. Please don't assume that the more you get better, the more gear you need to improve. **This is simply inaccurate**.

Every single gear mentioned was personally tried and tested by me, but also was the choice of almost the 85% of the home recording world out there. I went and checked out every single review out there, lurking in forums, reading personal opinions and reviews, buying and comparing home recording gear and prices, so you won't have to.

Since opinions differ, it's pretty logical and I totally understand that some people will disagree with some of the gear. Please consider leaving a comment below and I would be happy to update the post. But please, don't forget the main purpose of this post, which is to **achieve as professional recordings as possible with the best value for money ratio**.

I won't take seriously, responses like "This $1.000 keyboard is way worse than that $50 keyboard". If you really believe that something that you read is wrong, then please say it. Be kind, explain the reasons behind your belief and offer value in general. Rude comments and personal attacks to other commenters won't be allowed.

It's time for me to say bye for now, if this post helped you in any way then consider subscribing to my newsletter, to give me permission to send you free lessons and tutorials. I send only free knowledge and only e-mails about home recording and music production.

If by any means you regret it in the future, there's a link in each and every email that gives you the option to unsubscribe with 1 click. There's no risk whatsoever. You have total control.

Liked what you read? Please help all home recording enthusiasts save their money and build a correct home recording studio setup by *sharing* this post below.

Thank you very much and please don't hesitate to join our forums, we're a group of music lovers that help each other achieve better recordings. Wish you a great day and happy recordings.

10. How To Master A Song At Home – Mastering Is Hyped [Controversial]

Welcome to the *How To Master A Song At Home – Mastering is Hyped* post. We'll talk about mastering music and I will share with you some personal opinions of mine about mastering audio.

Before I share with you my mastering tutorials I'd like to express some thoughts about mastering and first and foremost explain: *What is Mastering and we can really get professional results or is it pseudo-mastering, as many people say?*

Can we really get commercial sounding tracks with plugins or do we need to spend thousands of money for "proper mastering gear". **Hint:** We don't, but let's discuss.

Note: *This post is controversial and if you swear by analog gear, there's a slight chance you may get offended. If you'd like to skip the controversy you may jump to the tutorials or just continue reading.*

What Is Mastering?

When you read music forums you possible see the terms *Recording, Mixing and Mastering*.

While Recording is pretty self-explanatory and mixing is the process of making all the tracks working together as a team, volume-wise, dynamic-wise and frequency-wise, then why the heck do we need mastering for?

Mastering is the final "gloss" of your mix . It's the preparation of the track for the final tweaks. It's the stage where we've already exported our mix into 1 single WAV file and add our final touch on it, before we publish it.

If we take a car as an example, the recording stage is like finding the parts of the car – *great* parts of the track, mixing is the process of assembling them and making them work together, while mastering is like the final gloss to make it more shiny so you can deliver it.

As you can see, if we were to create a chain of importance it would be something like this: **Composition -> Recording -> Mixing -> Mastering**.

If you know how to find (record properly) or even **create from scratch** the parts of the car (sound design – creating great source sounds) and assemble them properly, then there's no way you will find some kind of difficulty to gloss it.

Mastering is Hyped

Now you may ask: *But , I see many people saying that Mastering is a totally different league and they're posting replies similar to the image below:*

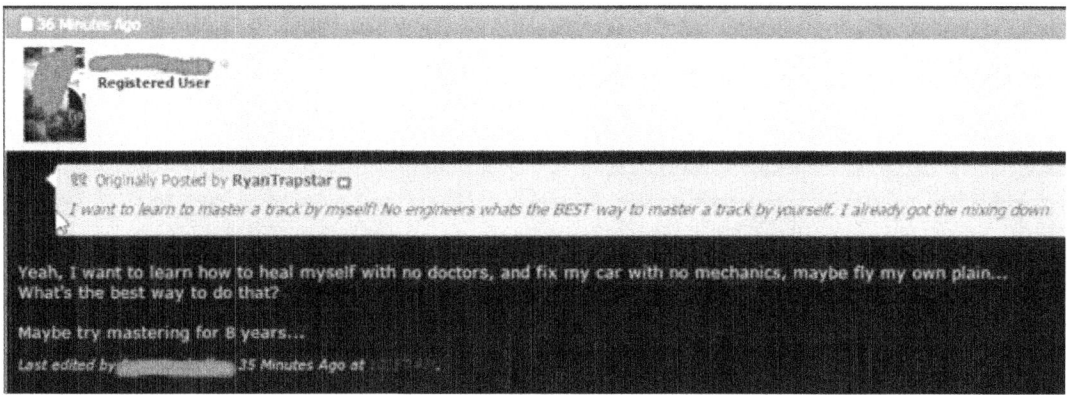

Mastering for 8 years. Really now. Try mastering for 8 years to achieve a great sound? 8 whole years of *mastering* to get a commercial sounding track?

Aw well, sorry but I can't resist:

Before you think I'm against mastering, allow me to clear up some things, including that I know that mastering is not only about volume.

Mastering **is** needed. Mastering is a stage that a song can't live without. No one can argue with this. But give me a damn break.

Let's build a huge building. There are 1.000 employees there creating everything, working hard and smart. And then the CEO of the construction company just appears in the last 10% of the work and does his thing and says: "Look what I've created". Sure thing dude.

It's the same thing: You worked hard finding that sweet spot with your microphone on the guitar cabinet. You spent hours with your singer using multiple mics to find what's the one that complement her vocals most. You changed 4-5 guitars and 3-4 guitar and bass cabinets and microphones to find which are the most appropriate *according to the mix*.

You've spent 1 week sound designing with Sylenth to create a signature sound of your liking, playing with EQs, saturation, compressors, LFOs, sinewaves and such. You've recorded, mixed and in general you've produced the 90% of the product to send it to a mastering engineer and say:

"But mastering is a different league, you cannot understand what we've been through! And if you think it's easy the results are not the same with your plugins, we've spent thousands for our mastering gear!"

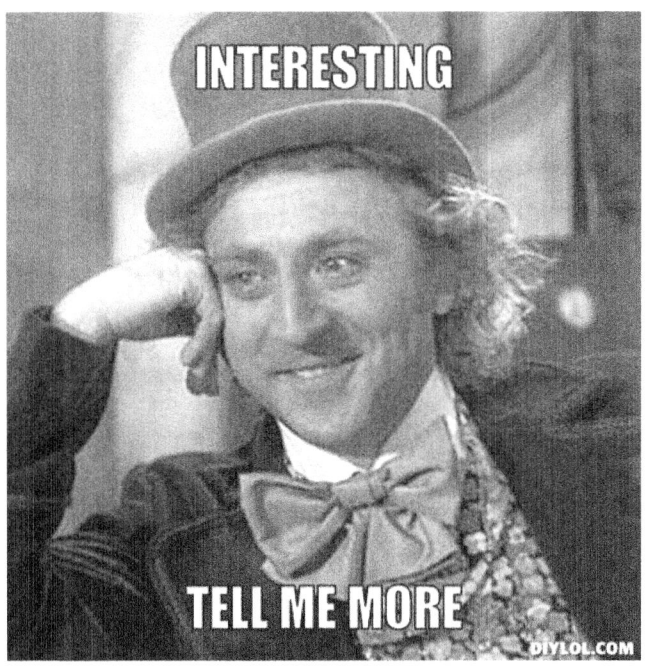

If someone had to "complain" about how hard is to produce a song, then the recording & mixing engineers are the ones that have the right to talk. Definitely not the exclusive mastering engineers.

While mastering needs experience to get it done, it's not a "different league". It's easier than sound-design, recording and mixing combined, so please stop playing with our IQ.

The Real Problem

The real problem of these stupid phrases, such as: *"Mastering is a totally different league"* and *"you need thousands of money to master properly",* is the fact that they spread mis-information and newcomers to home recording get the basics wrong.

Since I'd like to speak with proof… How many times have you encountered people saying " **Don't worry about recording man, we'll fix it in the mix!".** Then it becomes worse: *"Why are you trying to mix this stuff, we'll fix it in mastering!".*

But *some* mastering engineers keep on spreading the rumor that them and their gear is a necessity for a radio-ready song.

See where all this is going?

We give more weight to the less needed stages of a production and less weight to the most important ones.

I have nothing against exclusive mastering engineers. But I can't stand their stupid marketing that mastering is above recording and mixing combined, just for them to make back their thousands of $ spent for gear.

The sad part is that when I try to help people on forums and give them mixing advice I get responses such as: *"Hey thanks for taking the time to help, but I haven't sent my track to a mastering engineer yet, that's why it sucks".*

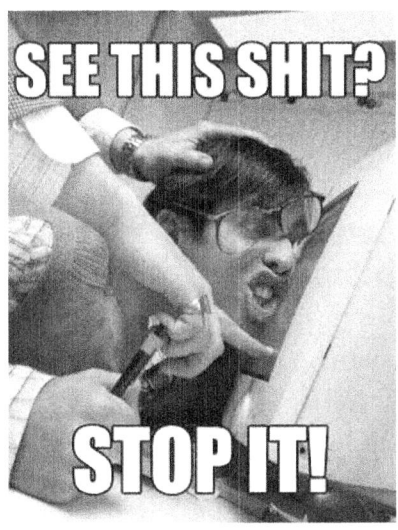

Guys, GUYS! Wake up and please stop worshiping mastering.
If you need to worship something at least start from *recording -> mixing*, and then you'll see mastering with a new perspective.

Just because not every single mastering engineer has this kind of mindset **(there are actually lots of ones which I admire and respect),** it's unfair to speak for mastering engineers in such general terms.

So, to make it fair for everyone I will split the mastering engineers into 2 basic groups based on their mindset. I will start from the mastering engineers with the mindset that I love and admire.

There Are Mainly 2 Groups of Mastering Engineers

The 1st group is the one that I respect most.

They are the ones that have the guts and decency to admit that *only back in the days when technology was not so advanced*, there wasn't a proper way to achieve commercial sounding results without analog gear.

Computer VST plugins were simply not good enough, they lacked lots of things comparing to their analog counterparts.

They lacked character, but most important, they sounded like s**t. Technology was simply not good enough for us to get decent results. There was not other way to get a professionally mastered song without a room filled with expensive analog gear.

This 1st group of these mastering engineers now, have the guts to admit that *some* of their analog gear can easily be replaced by *some* plugins. They even admit that they can do their job even faster with the mouse sometimes.

They have no problem to admit that they're not in need of a specific analog gear any more. They admit that they have made back their money – and a lot more – but they've got no problem to admit that it's time for some of their expensive gear **to retire**.

They go with the (technological) flow.

They are open minded and willing to listen and try out new things. They don't feel the need to defend their gear just because they have spent money on it.

If a plugin helps them fulfill their mission they'll use it and they won't complain about not using a gear that it's time to retire.

I would be also sad if a plugin that cost less than my $$$$ analog gear did the job fine, but I'd better accept the advanced technology and step up my game rather than crying and running A/B split tests of how "my" gear is "noticeably" better.

This group of mastering engineers, also have the guts to admit to the client that if his mix is completely s**t
and unfixable, he prompts them to mix again, cause no matter the quality of the mastering used on the track, it will stil sound lame.

The 2nd group of the engineers do the exact opposite. They won't give advice to the client and prompt him to re-mix for the best possible result.

Instead, they hope to get a sh**tty mix to be able to apply mixing principles during mastering, so that their before and after difference would be huge. This way they can brag about their mastering skills easier.

In this 1st group, we usually find successful mastering engineers, engineers that get nothing personal and continue doing what they know best, with everything, digital or analog. They will give you great results no matter if you let them use a plugin or an expensive compressor.

The 2nd Group

On the opposite side, we've got the **2nd group**. These mastering engineers take everything personally. They act like they have helped a company to create that *insert analog gear here*.

When you show them proof that *this* plugin can achieve the same results with *that* analog gear of theirs, they're getting mad and enter a defensive stance.

Chill out guys, you have not even played a part in the creation process of the gear. You just bought the damn thing, don't take it personally.

Even the companies themselves admit that they need to step up the game, so why are you getting so offended for something that you haven't even created?

If it's the fact that audio companies have finally reached to the point of creating quality sounding plugins that do the same job as some of your analog gear, but way cheaper and way easier to use (free room space), then it's time to admit it and just step up your game too?

In this 2nd group, we usually find strong, narrow-minded opinions that swear to god that their analog gear is way better than the "bad" and "fake" plugins.

They call the mastering achieved by plugins **pseudo-mastering,** and for them, "real" mastering can only be achieved by using expensive high end stuff.

When you ask them to prove their sayings and give you some audio samples to listen to, they either get offended and change subject. Out of the ones that agree to do it, you just compare their mastered tracks to the 1st group of the engineers with theirs…

Trust me, what really sounds like pseudo-mastering is not the 1st group's tracks. * *wink wink* *

P.S: If you felt mad or got offended while reading this section about the 2nd group, I've got some bad news for you

The One And Only Benefit of Hiring A Mastering Engineer

Now that I've dug myself a hole with all this negativity & controversy, I guess it's time for me to admit something really positive about hiring a mastering engineer.

This is nothing else by just *getting a slightly different version of your song* . Maybe with a bit more bass or with less bass, with a bit louder or softer vocals. That's it. You will just get a *different perspective and feeling of your song*, from the personal point of view of the engineer.

Does that mean it will sound better than yours? Nope. Just different. It really depends on taste. You might love it and worship the perspective of the mastering engineer or hate it and wonder why you've even trusted him and spent your money.

The above things only take place when you know at least the basics of mixing & mastering.

If you have never in your life tried to master and you're scratching your head about it, then chances are that the mastering engineer *will* improve your song.

If you know how to mix though and you've created a specific sound in your mind, then just master it yourself. The mastering engineer can't enter your brain and you can't make him master just the way you want him to.

He will master with his own influences and taste – and that's the beauty of hiring a mastering engineer.

A great master starts with a great mix, which starts with great recording, which starts with great composition.

If you mixed perfectly, then just use mastering for loudness and for some gentle glue compression. More of this will make your mix worse. There's a golden rule for mastering and that is: **Don't fix what's not broken.**

This is also a trap that many people that outsource mastering fall into.

They might have mixed a really FANTASTIC mix, so great that the only thing it needs is just a maximizer. But since they have been convinced that without "analog real" stuff the song will suck, they decide to bite the bullet and hire a mastering engineer.

A correct mastering engineer will recognize the *don't fix what's not broken* rule and will just give the mix what it needs just a maximizer, since frequency-wise is perfect.

A wrong mastering engineer will just make it different, even worse sometimes, but definitely different in order to justify the money he will get.

And that's usually the trap many people fall to. They give a perfectly balanced mix and they get back a worse one, but louder. And since our ears love loudness, they believe that it's better.

If they remove loudness and compare their un-mastered mix with the mastered one, they will say WTF is this s**t? No thanks you keep it, I'll keep mine and just add a maximizer!

How To Master A Song At Home

In this section, I will post my mastering tutorials, feel free to watch them in 1080p **here**.

I will post more in the near future so feel free to subscribe for free to my newsletter if you wish, on the right of your screen, so I can update you.

This post won't be updated, but I will update this mastering tutorials category for sure! It's the category where I keep all the mastering tutorials nice and tidy.

Final Verdict

If you're sure that you know what you're doing recording-wise and mixing-wise then you can easily learn to master your own songs.

Recording and mixing is like learning how to walk and run. Mastering is like running... *just a tad faster*. There's nothing extraordinary new you will encounter during mastering if you are – I repeat – 100% sure that you know what you're doing during recording & mixing.

If your mixing skills need improvement and you're not sure about them, then diving into mastering might get you more confused than you might are.

Just focus on improving on recording and mixing, do your things, **finish mixing projects** and hire mastering engineers *until you're sure that you know what you're doing* .

When you reach to the point that your mix will only need a bit of loudness and maybe some glue compression, then you will feel sure that you will have mastered your mixing skills – see what I did there? Master your mixing skills...?

No? Ok

Again, when your mix feels like it has reached 90% of completion, then you will have truly grasped the principles of each processor (compressors, EQs, Reverbs, etc). And if you do that, you can easily fill up the remaining final 10% of your project (a.k.a Mastering) by yourself.

11. How To Promote Your Music on YouTube Effectively

How To Get Real & Targeted YouTube Views and Subscribers –
On Autopilot

*"This guide is **not** about buying fake views or any other kind of similar actions"*

Introduction

In this guide, I am going to show you how to get Real YouTube Views & Subscribers to your videos and promote your youtube channel – on autopilot.

This guide is NOT about buying fake views and subs. We're talking about 100% Real people that will:

Comment on your videos Subscribe to your channel
May watch your ads – if you've enabled them

Keyword Targeted – they will be interested in your subject, no matter what.

Active Youtubers – We'll engage people that have commented on videos similar to yours and are proven to be **a)** interested in your content **b)** active youtubers – because they're active in the comment section.

You won't even have to open your computer for this to work. It's just a set and forget method.

This is 100% Adsense Safe. Even if you are a certitied youtuber, this is going to work. You don't need to be a tech- savvy person in order to make this work.

What we're going to do is as easy as turning on our computer.

I highly recommend you follow the steps with me. I've also added images to make it even easier for you to follow along.

I know you're here to make your channel noticeable so… Let's get started, shall we?

Pro Tip: At the end of this guide you can find proof that this is working for my personal channel. I even log in to prove that's it's actually mine. Let's continue

1. Target Your Audience

For this example, I pretend to be a hip hop producer that wants to promote his hip hop track. I want to target people that search on youtube: **best hip hop songs**

You can use any kind of keyword, depending on your situation. If you want to promote your channel with make up tutorials then do this:

Type **make up tutorials** and **do not** hit Enter.

You'll see youtube giving you some keywords that most people search.

Choose **5** of them – choose the ones that you think will work best. It's really easy, all you have to do is to think like a visitor/customer that are looking for your videos.

Take me as an example…

I typed **best hip hop songs** and I chose these 5 keywords:

   1. best hip songs 2014

2. best hip hop songs

3.
best hip hop songs 2015 – *this is missing from the list but I am sure it will get more views since we are on 2015 now*
4. best hip hop 2015

5. best hip hop 2014

These are some keywords that my audience is searching.

These are ultra-targeted keywords, meaning that people are actually looking for my video and I will just simply give them what they're looking for.

2. Create A Free Account

TubeAssist is the system we're going to use that is accepted by youtube and is used by thousands of certified YouTubers.

Plus, it was built from the ground up following *YouTube's TOS* and runs using their *public programming API* . You can't get safer than this.

3. Connect Your YouTube Account(s)

In order to connect your account, all you have to do is to click **Add -> I have the Channel login & password**, as shown in the image above.

I've connected 3 youtube accounts of mine, but I greyed them out for obvious reasons

When you click the "**I have the Channel login & password**" button, youtube will ask your permission to add your account to TubeAssist.

This is proof that YouTube recognizes tubeassist and the fact that they can work together shows the legitimacy of this system.

For this step to be completed, just click **accept/allow** everything YouTube is asking for, so the communication between them can start flawlessly.

4. Set Up Your Campaigns

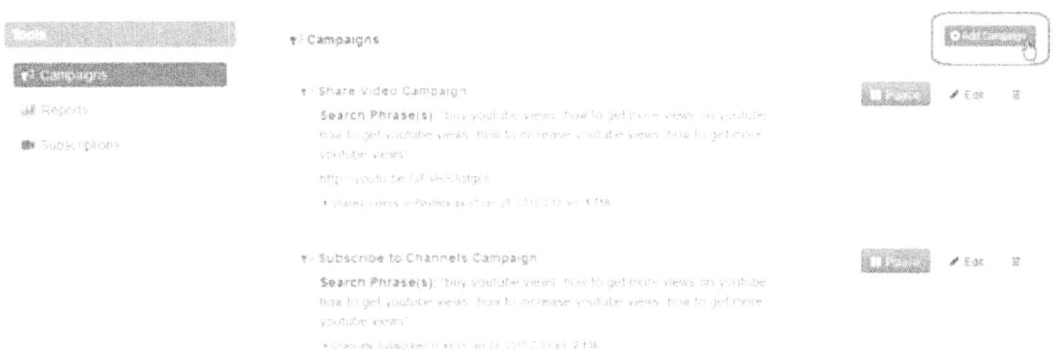

Click **Add Campaign** as shown in the image above.

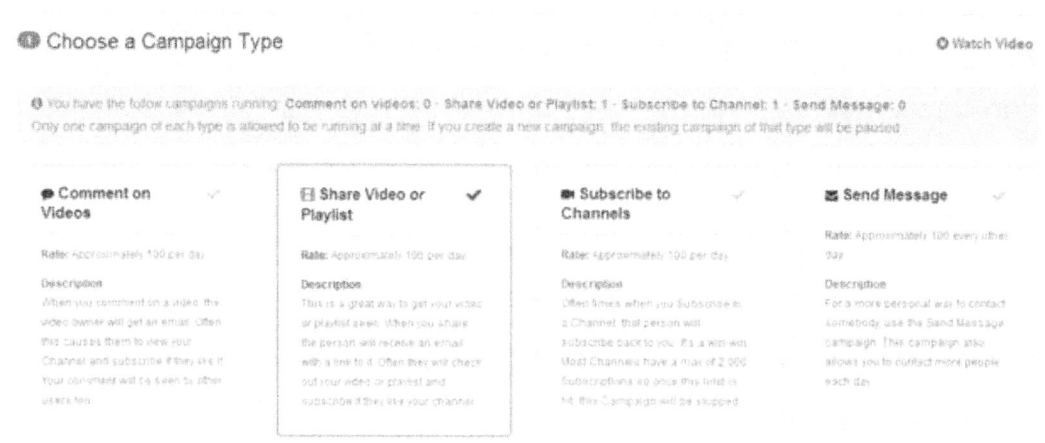

There are **4 campaigns**. Each account can use all of them at once (optional).

For now, we're going to use the most used one and my personal favorite. **Share Video or Playlist** is my absolute favorite.

I am going to guide you how to set up this one and the other ones work the same with some minor differences, that I'll also explain in a moment.

So click **Share Video or Playlist** and you'll get this image:

Remember the keywords we got before?

Now it's time to copy-paste them in the fields. Yes, it's that easy. Let's move on!

Now, all we have to do is to select our video from the **My Video** field – since your account is connected the videos will be waiting for you to select them.

Alternatively, you can copy-paste the URL of your video, but I believe the 1st option is easier.

4.b. Messages

Now it's time to add our **Message.**

I use a formula that works pretty much for every video/keyword and it's proven to make people click and watch your video (that's what we want right?) and I'm going to share the formula with you, right now.

The Message:

Hey, I see you're interested in and I'd be excited if you could check out mine – I put lots of hard work to it! You can check it out here:

The Message with my Hip Hop Example:

Hey, I see you're interested in **hip hop songs** and I'd be excited if you could check out mine – I put lots of hard work to it! You can check it out here:

You can easily change this, it does nothave to be the exact same message but please pay attention to some critical points:

It's not boring and gets to the point

It's got a CTA (Call To Action) sentence in the end.

Words like "check it out here" , "watch my video here" , "Comment here" are call-to-action sentences and they improve clicks dramatically.

A fantastic trick to add to the message:

You can also make TubeAssist post a different message, plus keeping the meaning the same. How can you do that?

It's really easy... You just tell it to use a different synonym randomly. This will generate lots of sentences. For example, we can tell it to post:
Hey **OR** Hi **OR** Hello there **OR** What's up...

If we replace **OR** with this symbol **|** (which still means **or**) we get something like this: Hey | Hi | Hello there | What's up
Now let's use brackets to close the sentence.

{ Hey | Hi | Hello there | What's up **}**

Now tubeassist knows that each time it will need to post a message, it will generate randomly a new sentence. Pretty cool, isn't it?

But don't worry, you don't have to add all these synonyms by yourself. I've done all the hard work for you. Just copy – paste the text below

Here's the full and final message including the synonyms:

{Hey|Hi|Hello there|What's up|Hello}, I {see|can see} you're {interested in|serious about|enthusiastic about|excited by|intrigued by|excited about} **hip hop songs**, and {I'd|I would|i will} be {thrilled|happy|excited} if {you could|you may|you may choose to|you could possibly|you are able to|you could actually|you might} check out mine – I put lots of
{hard work|time and effort|dedication|time and energy} to it! You can check it out here:

Just replace **hip hop songs** and add your own subject/keywords and copy-paste it in the **Message** field. Feel free to change the message a bit If you feel you'll get more clicks/views to your video, but don't forget to use a Call-To-Action word.

Always be gentle and kind, but to the point.

Click **Save Changes** and go for a walk, watch a movie or anything you'd love to do.

5. Explaining The Differences Of Each Campaign

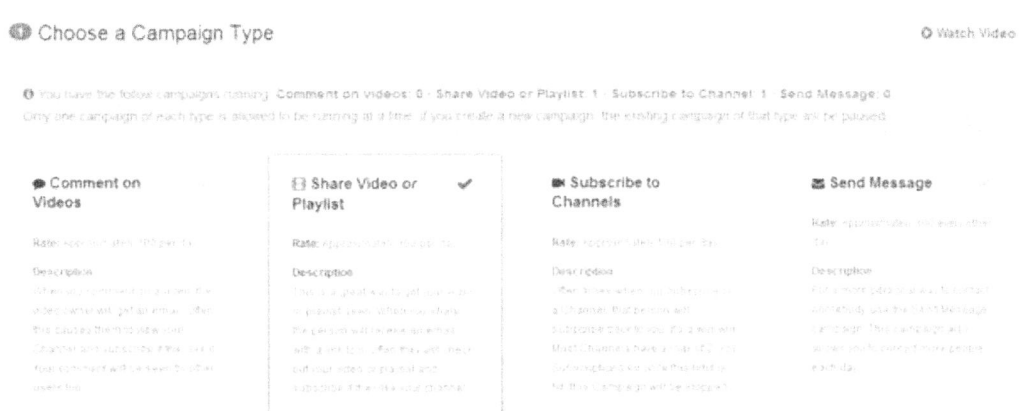

Share Video or Playlist: My absolute favorite and a must. Connects with your targeted viewers direct

Comment on Videos: This is just like *the share video or playlist* campaign, but it comments in public. This can bring lots of extra targeted people to your video and works even greater with the tip I showed you above. You can set this up the same way you do with the *Share Video or Playlist* campaign.

Subscribe to Channels: People subscribe back when you subscribe to them, thus you get more views and attention. You can set this up and if someone won't subscribe back in 2 weeks, tubeassist automatically removes them! You can also make it remove them even if they do subscribe back, but I consider this a bad move, so I always select to stay subscribed if they do to.

Send Message: This is a brand new feature that I don't normally use. It's like the *Share Video or Playlist campaign* but it gives you 60 more posts per day, but the only drawback is that you need to have your computer on , while the others are 100% on the cloud.

Did I mention anything about the internal anti-spam system?

Well, when you send something to someone it gets added to a "do not bother" list, so he won't be contacted again **plus** each campaign allows ~360 connections per day.

It will not surpass this 360 to 450 per day limit, because it's built that way to comply with youtube's TOS. Absolutely amazing.

Proof

I am a person that loves to show proof, so I am going to show you that this is working.

You know, my main love is to make people aware of stuff that will improve their life, but this isn't my one and only love I am a also a music producer, rock/metal and epic-cinematic music fan (you know the kind of music we hear on trailers) and I thought…

"Since I know my job so well, why don't I use youtube to make some extra money by helping others for free? I'd love to help others for free! But I 've got one problem though… I've got no marketing knowledge and I'll have no views and even if I had the knowledge to do so… I have no time 'cause I can't stop composing music – I need to find something that's effective and does everything on autopilot".

And then I've found this perfect solution, so I could reach you guys and let you know about my free lessons.

I set up my campaigns and these are some of the comments I've got from people:

Jeff Kambale Mathe 3 mor"'s ago

Thank so much for sharing this link with me Ihave enjoyed the tutorial h is enlightening Will surely apply the tips.Questions .will
of the tips work for other DAW or is it JUSt for Cubase?
Thanks .

Reply

Hide replies ""

I. 'r•ont .,...   0

+Jeff Kamlh111e Mathe Of course my fnend rt doesn' matter what daw you're using the basic things that change are the
shortcuts a'ml the interface. apart from these 99% are the same!

Reply   tf Jt

CHILLhard 2 l"lonths a <o

sweetttt,thanks for making this and bringing my attention to it by commenting on my vid best tutorial

Repy

View 1reply v

Rohan Herath 2 weeks ago   <:!:•

•

Hi thank yo• !for showing this tutorial and send a link specially.But I cant cant understand what this programme? Is it video editing software? I'm a videographer and a photographer. Ijust started leaning the video editing and I am so ammeture when Iwatch your link. If you can help me little bit more it will be great. Thanks

tf "

Reply

Hide replies .-..

I. 2 weeks ago
This is cubase.It's made for music production :) EQualizers,Compressors,Reverbs and Delays are the 4 most used
"effects " / processors used to record and mix music :)

Reply ·

Fusion Music 2 weeks ago
Rohan, If Iwere you,Iwould just stick with a Video Editing software.You can change the volume(s) of each audio track and also change the tones (eq). You can cut words out if you need to . Get used to your video software and photography first before you get into audio in a big way. Audio is exciting , but if you don't understand it,you may be better leaving it alone or Read more

Reply ·

I. 6days ago
+Fusion Music Couldn't have said this better than you,thanks :0

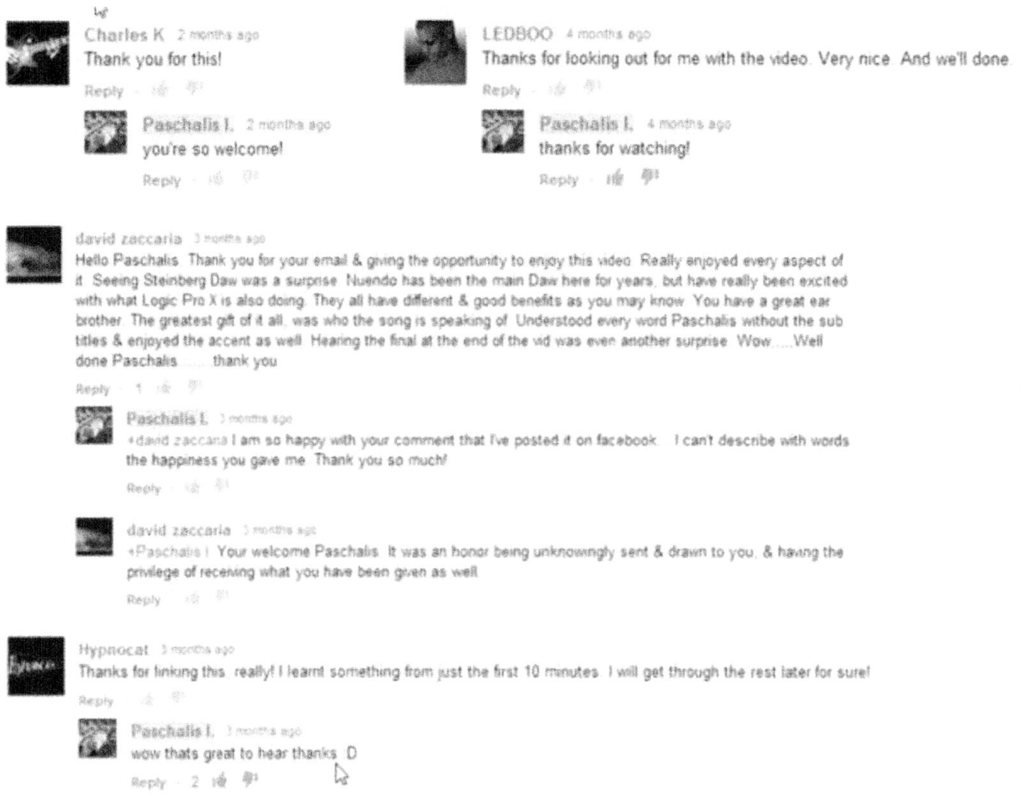

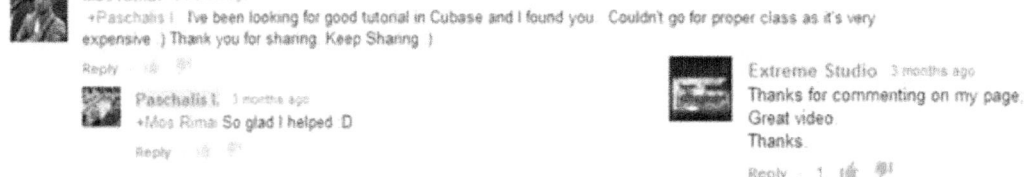

As you can see these are **some** comments of people that have been connected directly with me without me doing no promotion at all, but rather spending my time creating free lessons for you, while other people are trying to rank for keywords.

Ranking for keywords takes weeks or even months.

I am not saying that ranking for keywords is a bad thing, actually I find it to be a good thing but… We are always trying to rank while we forget the most important stuff. Connect with others!

We 're humans, we have languages, we have minds, we can **communicate**.

We tend to over-complicate things for no reason, while the solution is right in front of our eyes.

Talking about ranking...

People are spending tons of money to rank for keywords. I know it seems crazy but they do.

The competition out there is huge and people are acting like wolves stalking their prey (keywords) so they can get the best possible traffic.

They're trying to "trick" the youtube ranking algorithm by sending fake views, favorites and likes.

So that youtube thinks that a video is more popular than another, since it's getting views, thus place it higher in the search results.

I was always against that, ranking is tempting, but I find this unfair for others.

Not only that, but what if my "ranking procedure" failed miserably and all of my money went straight to trash?

Or even worse… What if youtube finds out that I am trying to trick the algorithm and ban my video? These are the most used reasons I will never buy fake views and better stick to websites like TubeAssist that's officially approved by youtube. Better stay safe!

But you know what? I got ranked on 1st Page!

Since I engaged my viewers directly and saw real views coming on my video, I outranked the other videos with their fake views.

You know why?

'Cause of my real comments!

Youtube was fed up with all of these videos with fake views and no comments and **changed their ranking algorithm** – (I saw some improvement in my videos and googled about it).

Now it does not matter if you've got THOUSANDS of views – it doesn't matter!

Youtube now ranks your videos according to your **video activity**. Real comments now beat thousands of fake views! Well done youtube!

And for the above reason, I ranked for a keyword that I would be thrilled to be on page 1. Check this out:

Update: This picture below is old, now I'm not 4th in position on 1st page, but I'm 2nd in position on 1st page!

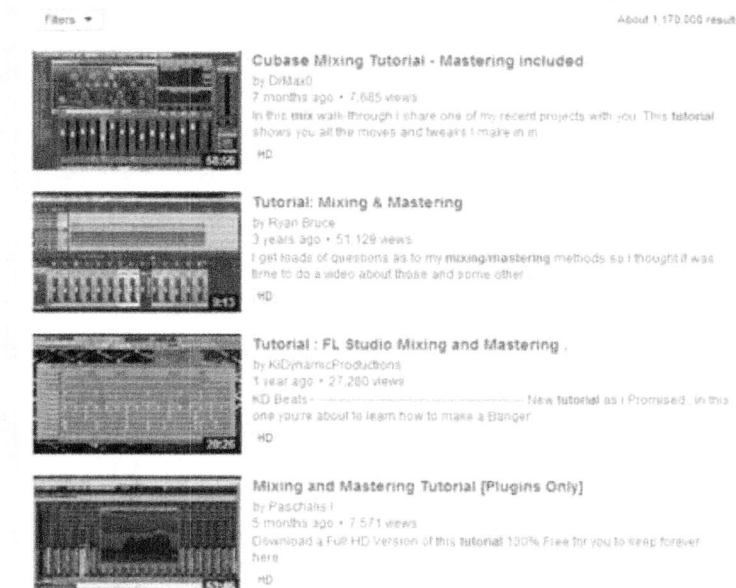

I rank 4th (old now ranking 2nd) .

Not bad for 0 work from me, since tubeassist does all the work for me on autopilot!

Mission Complete: Now I can spend all my time mixing, composing and creating free tutorials for you and I've got something really cool that notifies you about my free lessons.

And there you have it.

My whole marketing strategy in a step-by-step Guide. Let's sum up…

To Sum Up – We're Talking About:

100% Real Views & Subscribers – Not *real-looking* ones but real. You're going to receive real comments too.

Keyword Targeted Viewers – If you're targeting people that are searching, for example, "best new pop songs" you can do thi It works for any keyword of your liking, of course.

Doesn't Use Up Any Resources On Your Computer – Shut down your pc (or mac). It will still work for you 24/7.

Markets Your YouTube Channels While You Sleep – Spend your time on better things rather than spending it on youtube marketing… (family, vacation, movies, beer with friends, etc).

100% Safe – This is used by thousands of certified YouTubers and was built from the ground up following

YouTube's TOS and runs using their *public programming API* . Can't get safer than this. Copyright © 2015   I. | All Rights Reserved

12. How To Record On Cubase – The A to Z Guide

Recording on Cubase is easier than you think, so in this tutorial I will show you how to record on cubase by keeping it easy and simple.

I will also show you how to record real instruments using **WAV** files (guitars, bass, drums etc) but I will also show you how to record using **MIDI**.

Also, click here to open a new tab, filtered with results about everything cubase related. Let's get started!

1. Configure Your Audio Interface

After the installation of your audio interface – no matter if it uses USB or Firewire connection – Cubase is now able to recognize it. The only thing you've got to do is to choose it.

Open Cubase and click on **Devices -> Device Setup.**

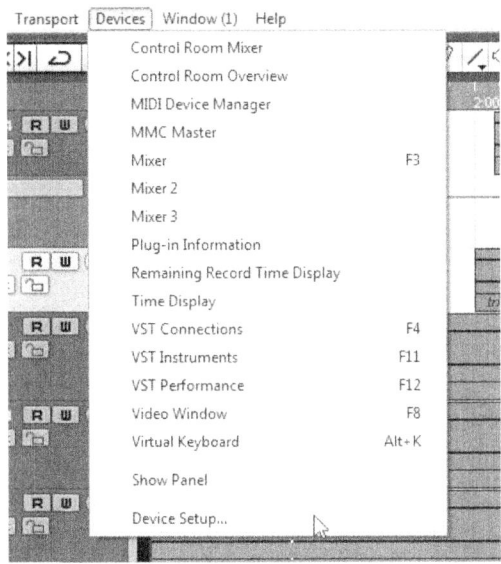

Then click on **VST Audio System** and choose your (already installed) audio interface.

The place that I create the tutorials is at my home. So I needed to get a cheap sound card at home for your recording and mixing tutorials. For this reason I about a $149 sound card the Focusrite Scarlett 2i2.

It's pretty logical to install it first in order for cubase to "see" it, else you won't be able to find it in the list below. Please choose your sound card and click **OK**.

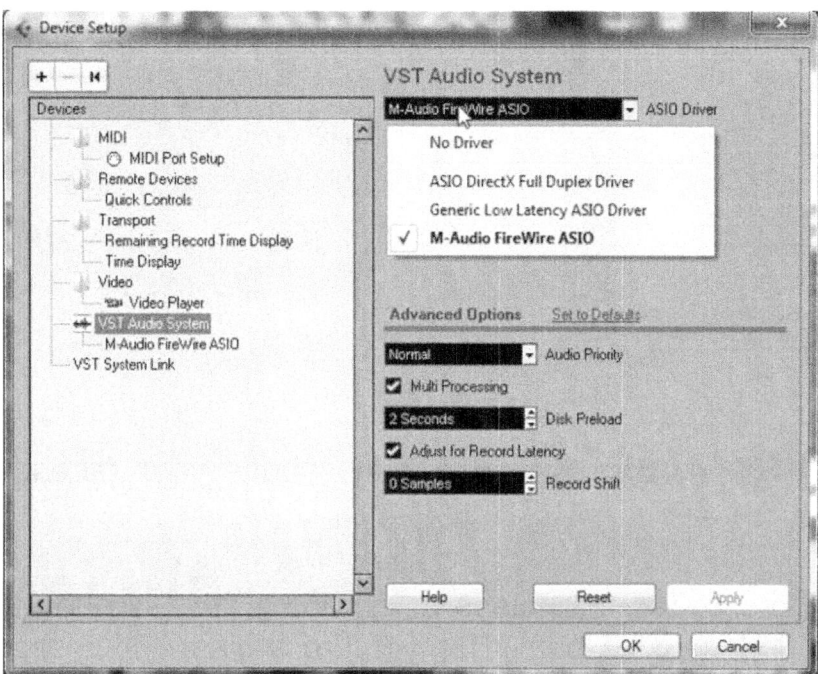

2. Configure Your VSTs

Before we create any channels it would be wise to configure our VST folder. Click on **Devices -> Plug-in Information**.

Now click on **VST** 2.x **Plug-in Paths**

And now c:lic:k **Add** to let Cubase know the folder that you will save your VSTs to.

As you c:an see there are some default folders but you c:an also create your own folder (palh).

Now, everytime you are going to install a new VST **you will choose the path that you've just created during the setup wizard**. Everything will be organized your own way!

This step is really a matter of preference.

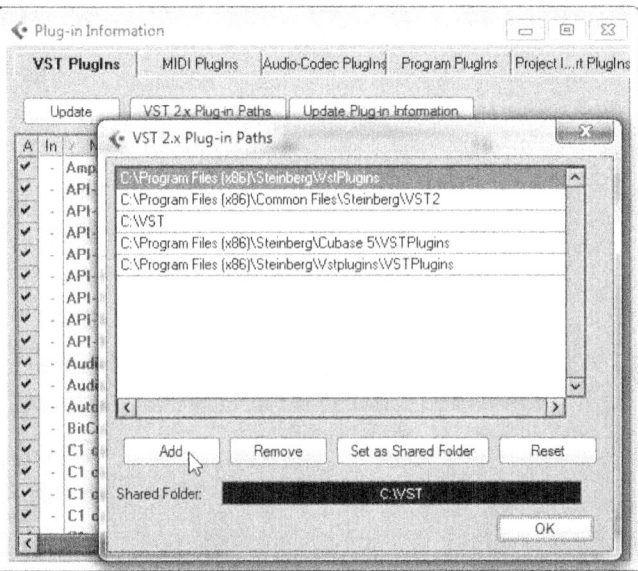

When you choose the folder/path of your liking just click on **OK** and then **Update**.

3. Create New Project

Click on **File -> New Project...**

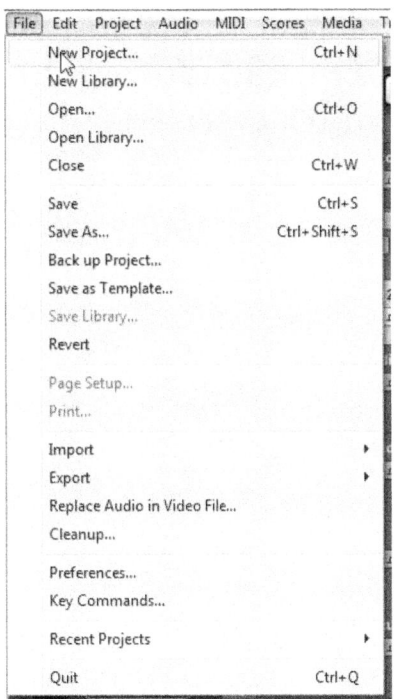

And now on **Empty**.

Choose the folder of your liking (the one that you are going to save the current project) and click **OK**.

class="calibre2" style="margin:0pt; border:0pt; height:1em">

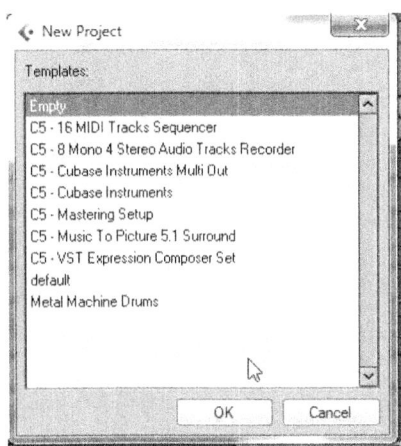

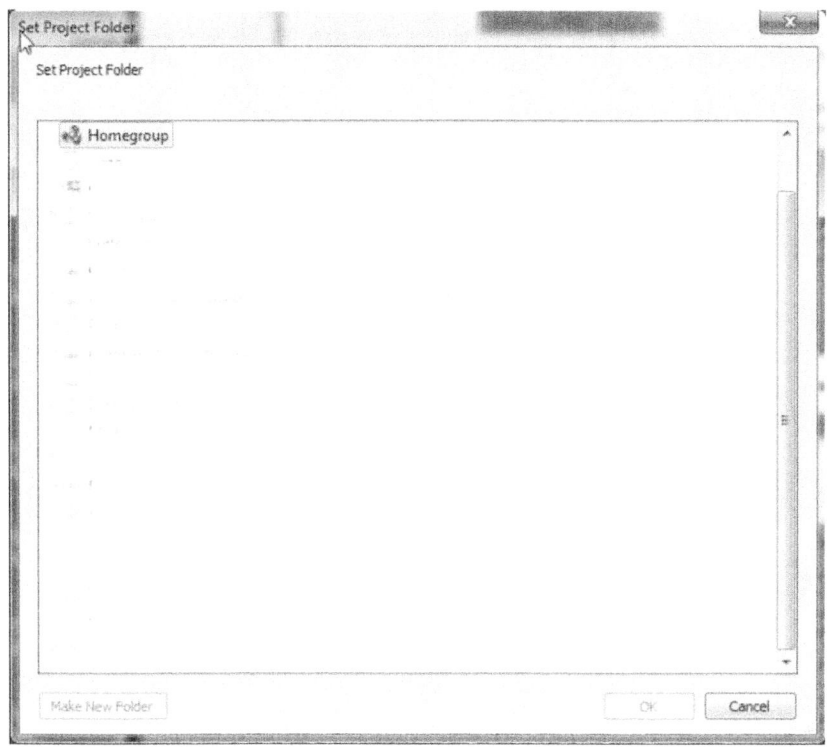

Then click on **File -> Save** and save the Project **in the same folder that you've just created above.**

4.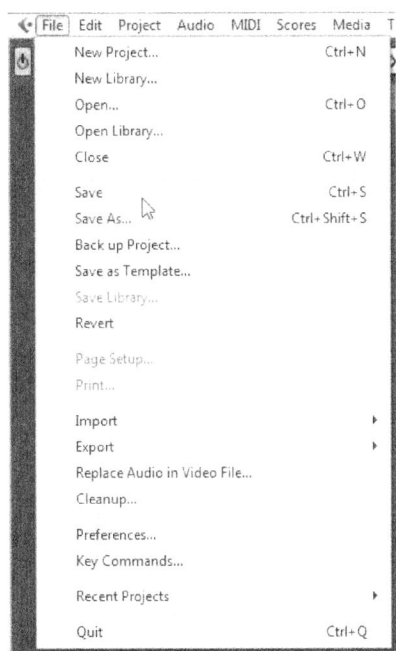

Recording WAV Audio Tracks

(Check out Step 6 for MIDI, but please read this chapter first)

When you save your project you'll end up with an empty screen of cubase without a track, but just the cubase tools.

Before we create our audio tracks, let me first explain the difference between Stereo and Mono Track.

Stereo VS Mono Track

The Stereo Track is nothing more than 2 Mono Tracks panned 100% Left and Right. If you send those 2 Mono Tracks to a single Group then you've got a Stereo Channel.

Then why do Stereo Tracks exist;

It's really simple. Because there are music programs that produce ready-made stereo sounds and in this case you don't need to record 2 Mono Tracks to create your Stereo Track/Sound.

Also, if there weren't any Stereo Tracks you wouldn't be able to process Multiple Mono Sounds in 1 Stereo Track/Group.

So, instead of sending multiple Mono Tracks to 1 Stereo Group Track and process that track, you would need to process each track individually **even if you used the exact same VSTs with the exact same settings** .

This results in spending double or even triple CPU power – in case you're mixing digitally – and of course spending more of your time to copy paste your equalizers, compressors, reverbs, etc.

So it's better to mix using the 1 Stereo Track and not the 2 Mono Tracks;

There's no difference and it's clearly depending on your computer's CPU power and RAM.

If you've got a strong PC/MAC that can handle lots of VSTs then work with the 2 Monos. You have more freedom this way.

Let me explain.

For example, a client can send me an instrument recorded on a Stereo Track and from my left speaker… it's a mess!!! My only option to fix problems is to work on this Stereo Track since I don't have access to both of the speakers (2 Mono Tracks panned hard left/right).

If I had access to the 2 Mono Tracks I could just edit the left mono track and not even touch the right speaker/microphone (because each Mono Track is recorded using different takes, so the signal of the microphone is different).

What I like in Pro Tools is that when you insert a Stereo Track it automatically separates them to 2 Monos panned 100% L and R for the reason that I just explained. It's just a matter of ¨workflow freedom¨.

Finally, without Stereo Tracks whatever Stereo Sound that you would "drag and drop" in the software for mixing, it would be converted to Mono… and I don't think you would like that!

Create Mono Audio Tracks

Now that we know the differences let's create our Tracks!

Right Click on the empty space and then click on **Add Audio Track**.

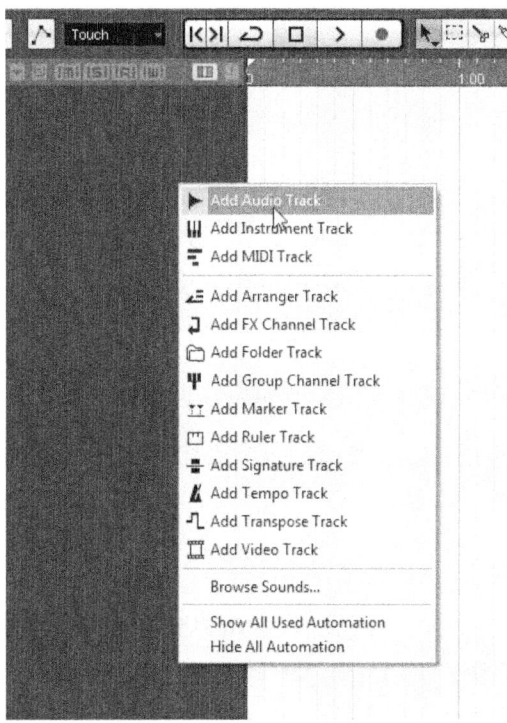

Choose **Mono** (unless you have an analog synthesizer, a VSTi Synth or anything that produces Stereo Audio) and then click **OK**.

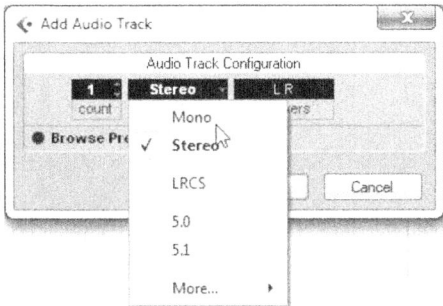

Highlight your **Track** and select your audio interface input. It should be the input that you've connected your microphone or instrument.

Depending on the sound card you would come across different options.

The sound card that I have at home has only 2 Inputs so there are only 2 choices – **Left** και **Right**.

I've connected the microphone to my left Input so I've chosen **Left**. Please choose your own input.

Arm the channel **(click the small red button).**

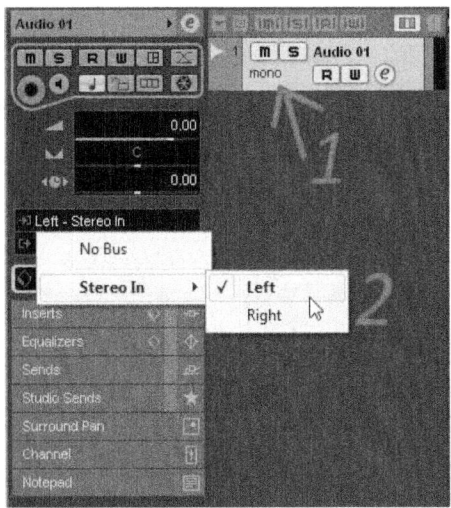

This "tells" Cubase that "When I'll press the Big Red Recording Button I want you to record this channel".

You can **Arm** many channels depending on how many Inputs your sound card has.

If you can connect, for example, 3 instruments you are able to record all 3 at the same time, by **arming all the 3 channels**.

If you want to the **Arm** button to be displayed on every simple track for faster movements then click the little arrow just like the image below.

Now choose **Default** or **Recording – Minimal**. When recording you are also able to hear the sound
you're recording coming out of your speakers
(Playback). Click on the **small orange Monitor Icon**
just like in the image below.

It's not necessary to have the monitor icon enabled in order to record though. **Arm** is for recording and **Monitor** is for listening to what you're recording.

Small Tip:

You usually use them together, but some home studio owners don't have enough room space, so they are obliged to put the guitar cabinet with the recording microphone next to the speakers. In this situation there's no need to enable monitoring.

Then click **Channel** to see the volume balance.

The recording volume can be configured from the "Gain" knob of your sound card and not by the channel itself.

The channel fader must be at it's default position just like the image below (if you are unsure about it just Control + Click the fader and it will return to its default position).

"Play" with your audio interface's **Gain** knob. Adjust it till the signal peaks at **-3db maximum**.

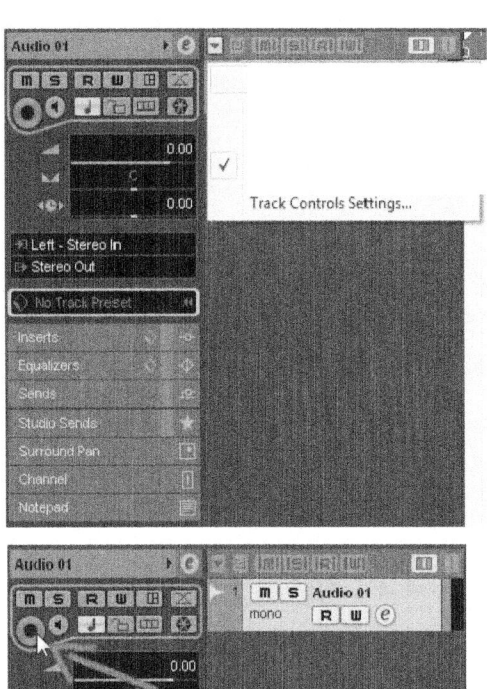

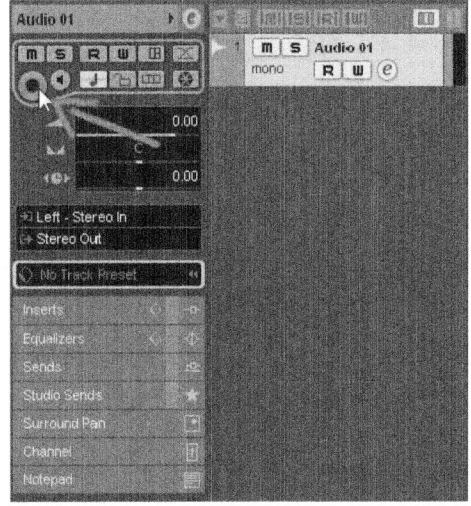

D"R_ult

Ret&rding - minimal

Editing

Mixing

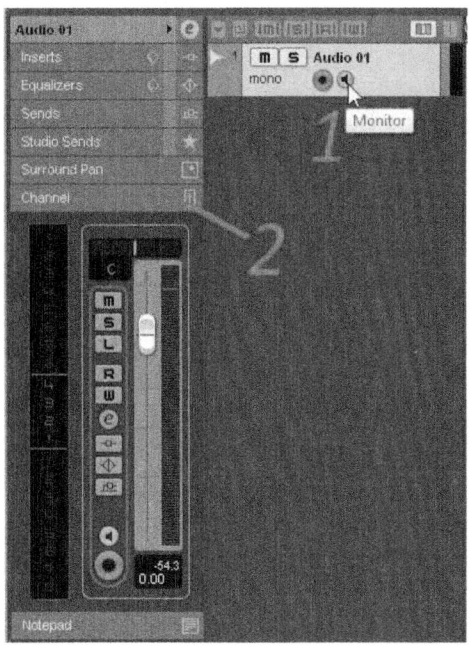

Before recording we should setup our song's **Tempo,** else it would be too late to change the tempo later!

Right Click on the empty space again and click **Add Tempo Track**.

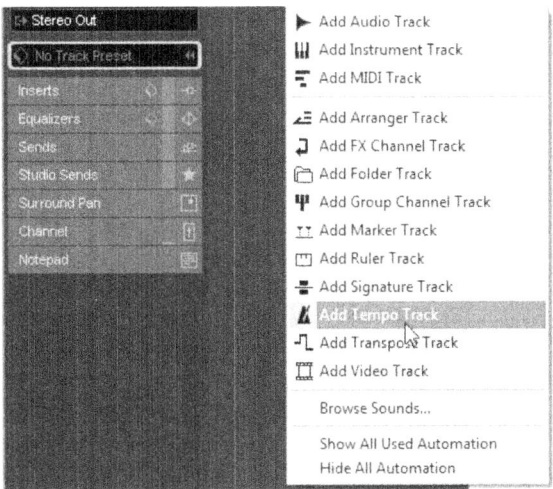

By clicking inside the bars you create new **Tempos** that you can adjust.

For example, if you want **Bar 5** to play on **140bmp** you just click on bar 5, create a new spot and **drag and drop this spot up and down to choose the bpm of your liking**.

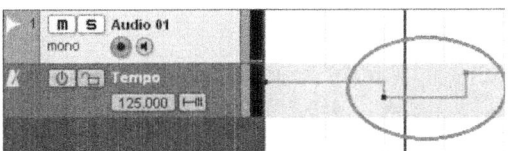

You can also hit **Ctrl + T** to open a new window with your Tempo Track and Zoom In. Don't forget to enable **Bars+Beats** and **Snap**.

Bars+Beats show you the bars of the song instead of time (minutes) and **Snap** "snaps" your clicks on the nearer bar for easier workflow.

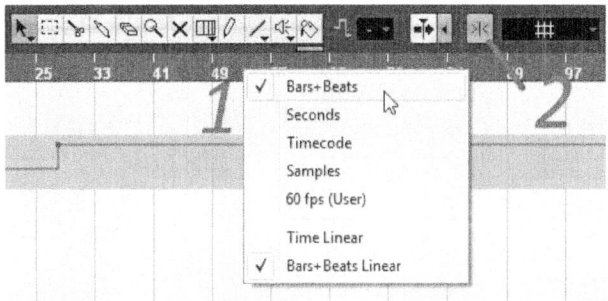

Also you need to Enable **Tempo Track** or Cubase won't take into consideration your configured BPMs.

Just hit **F2** and click like in the image below:

You've configured everything!

Just hit the big red button **(Record)**
and… Happy Recording!

You can stop recording by hitting
Space on your keyboard.

When you record your first take a new folder will appear – inside your saved project folder – with the name **Audio.**

DO NOT DELETE IT.

In there, you'll find all your **recording takes** and deleting it is not a good idea.

5. Play With Metronome

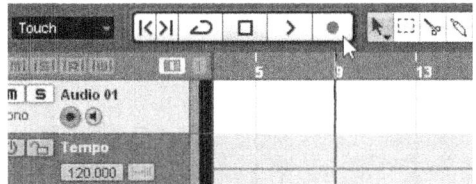

No Mixing Engineer can save a bad recorded song.

I am sure you know that there are tools to fix time issues but there's nothing better than working with experienced musicians and perfectly recorded takes.

Enable The Metronome

Just hit **F2** click **ON** like in the image below. By **Control Clicking** we open a new
window with the **Metronome Options:**

Metronome in Record: Enables Metronome while Recording.
Metronome in Play: Enables Metronome when Hearing (Playback).

Precount Bars: Choose how many bars you want the metronome to play on, before recording.

This is perfect because it gives you the opportunity to give yourself some time before you start recording. It's like someone singing to you "1… 2… 3… 4…" just to "get in" right.

Audio Click: Here we can configure the volume of the Metronome.

We can also choose different volumes for **1 (Hi Pitch)** and for **2-3-4 (Low Pitch).**
Pretty Cool huh?

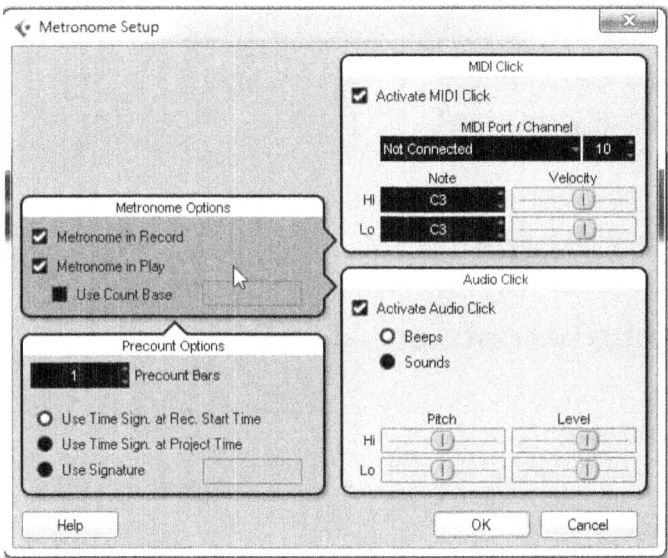

No matter the quantity of the **Precount Bars** that you've chosen, you also need to enable the precount bars.

Just click like in the image below to enable it.

6. Record MIDI

The way we record MIDI is almost the same with the way that we record WAV. The only difference is that now we are going to create MIDI tracks.

I will use a Cubase VST of my liking but if you want to use a third party VST that you've paid for it, it's pretty logical to install it first before following the steps below.

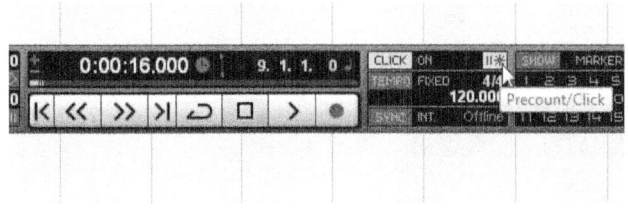

Recording Midi – The Steps

Click **Devices -> VST Instruments** or just hit **F11**.

Choose the software of your liking.

In this example I will use **EZ Drummer**.

Click **Create** on the window that will pop up.

A **MIDI** channel will appear that will get automatically get "connected" with your software/synth/VST. Choose the little **pencil tool (Draw)** or just hit **8** on your keyboard.
And **"draw"** on the bars that you want to compose music.

Change from the **pencil tool** to the little **arrow** by clicking it or by just hitting **1** on your keyboard. Now **Double Click** the box that you've just drawn.
In this window you can "draw" **notes** and also configure the **dynamics** of the notes.

Notes are displayed as **horizontal bars** and the dynamics as **vertical bars** at the bottom of your window. By selecting a box and hitting **Ctrl + D** (Duplicate) you create a duplicate box right next to the original one.

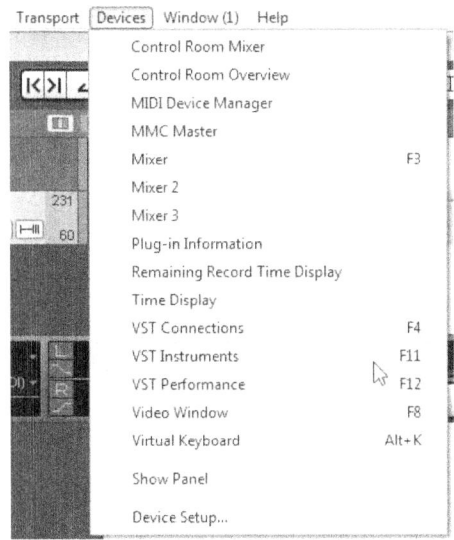

By clicking the **yellow piano icon** you can open your program's window.

If the program you're using has **more than 1 Outputs** hit **F11** again and Enable them, just like in the image below.

Some VSTi have only **1 output** which is always enabled by default.

On the contrary, there are many programs like the **EZ Drummer** that need more than 1 outputs/tracks (for the Kick, Snare, Hi-hat, Toms etc)

As you can see, with each **Output** that you enable
cubase also creates the corresponding track.

You're ready!

Now, **you can insert Effects and Processors on every single track!**

MIDI Track VS Instrument Track

Cubase also gives you the option to create **Instrument Tracks**.

What's their difference with the MIDI tracks? Is is better to use these Tracks or just follow the guidelines that I've shown you above?

The Difference Between the MIDI Track and the Instrument Track

The way of setting up the tracks that I showed you above is for me the most "correct" one. By what do I mean by correct?

Programs like EZDrummer and Nexus can produce more than 1 sounds. For example, EZDrummer, can produce multiple sounds like the Kick Drum, Snare, Toms, Overheads etc... so you need many outputs/tracks.

The way of setting up the tracks that I showed you above allows you to use every single program no matter how many outputs it needs.

No matter if you need 1 output or multiple outputs you are able to use everything.

On the contrary, the **Instrument Track** needs less clicks and less time to setup your software but it works only for software **that needs only 1 output.**

VSTi programs like piano, harp or bass can easily be used with the Instrument Track since you won't need multiple outputs/tracks.

As you can see, there's no "worse" or "better" track. It really depends on the program that you want to use.

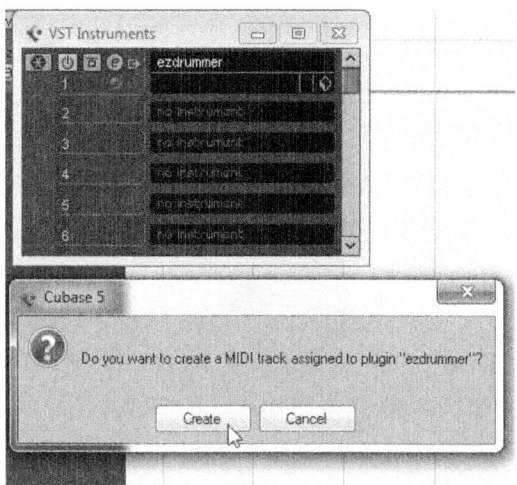

What I like to do is to use the **Instrument Tracks** on my bass VSTi – since it produces 1 sound, the bass guitar sound – and MIDI tracks on my Drum VSTi in case I want to blend some drum sounds with the drum sounds of my acoustic kit.

Let's See How To Setup A VSTi Program Using The Instrument Track

Right click on the empty space and then **Add Instrument Track**.

Choose a VSTi that needs **only 1 output** .

1. By clicking the little **piano icon** you open your program's interface window.

2. Click on **Inserts** to insert your VSTs there.

It's easier than it seems

I know that when you visited this page you thought "what is this thing?!".

The tutorial is a bit long yeah, but I would like to help you understand everything and not leave you with unanswered questions.

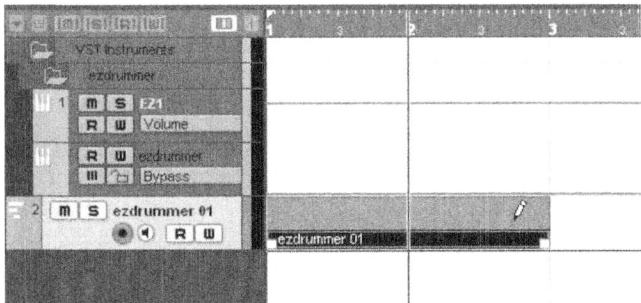

I guarantee that you will get used to it really fast.

Just follow step by step this tutorial and I am sure that you will be able to record without the help of this tutorial in just a couple of hours!

If you wanna thank me for this guide consider sharing this guide and leaving a comment below

Share some love for: How To Record On Cubase – The A to Z Guide.

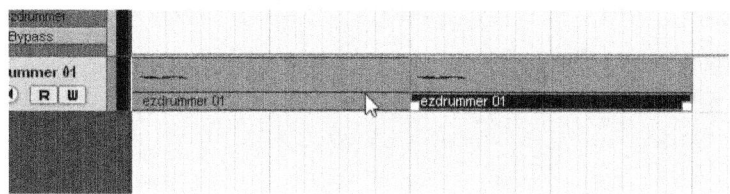

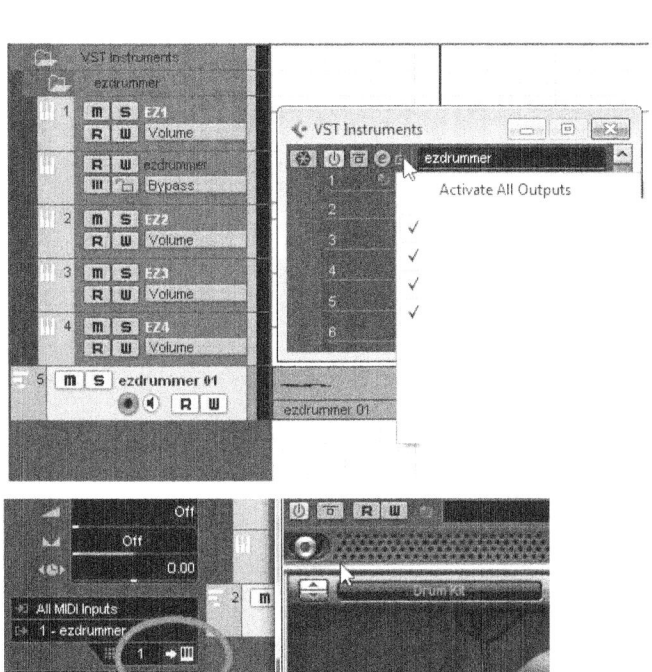

Ell [Stereo] EZ2 [Stereo] EZ3 [Stereo] EZ4 [Stereo] EZS [Stereo] EZ6 [Stereo] EZ7 [Stereo) EZ8 [Stereo]

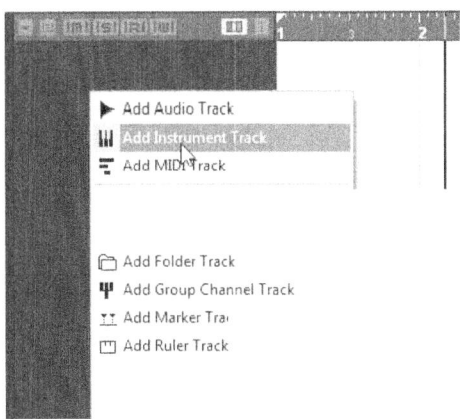

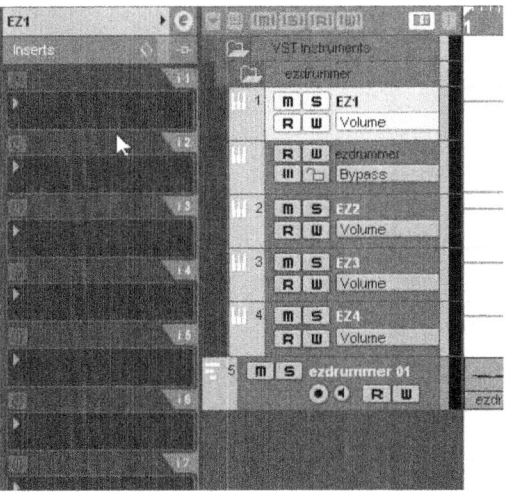

.,_: Add Arranger Track
J Add FX Channel Track

" Add MarkerTrack

:Add Signature Track
fJ. Add Tempo Track

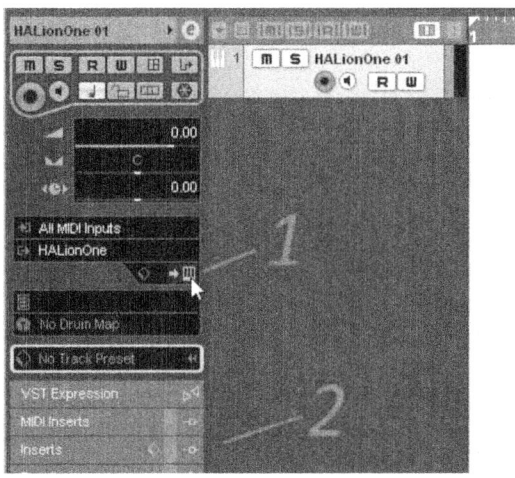

13. Midi Tutorial – For What Midi is Used For

In this midi tutorial we'll learn about MIDI, its purpose and its critical use on our productions.

Many people can't understand what it is and as a result they don't bother using it, which is a HUGE mistake.

It's a pity to leave this music opportunity known as MIDI so I will explain for what midi is used for in simple words.

Midi is nothing more than a signal (notes – usually played by a MIDI keyboard) that they don't have sound by themselves.

They "accept" a sound by using a second program specially designed to produce sounds using MIDI notes.

Let me explain…

Midi Tutorial – A simple explanation

I am sure you've seen a MIDI piano before. These are pianos that don't produce a sound unless we connect them to our computers via USB.

By using a recording software, we will be able to see to our monitor that the notes "flash" meaning that we've got a working signal but no sound coming from our speakers.
And here come the fantastic software that support midi to make our lives easier and our mixes… sounding fantastic! The programs are designed with a way so that they can receive the MIDI note and produce the sound that we are looking for.

Any. Simple. Sound!

We can produce anything we want like: bass sound, guitar sound or even **drums**!

How's that happening? You can adjust each midi note to product sounds from drums. For example, you can use the C Note as the Kick Drum, the D note as the Snare, the E note as the Hi-Hat and so on.

For the above reason you can play drums with just your midi keyboard.

There are countless programs that can easily help you get the professional you're looking for.

The sounds of the software are recorded in great sounding rooms using expensive and high quality recording equipment.

Then, using the power of the MIDI technology, you can get these sounds by installing the programs on your computer

Is it necessary to own a MIDI Piano?

No it's not.

The above example was just to help you understand the purpose of MIDI technology. All the recording software products support MIDI functionality and they have an **internal digital piano**.

This way you can "draw" the notes and compose music with **just some clicks of your mouse**!

Converting MIDI to WAV

When you open your favorite recording program no matter what you will use MIDI for (Drums, Bass, Synth, etc) you will be able to convert midi to wav.
Then you can drag and drop this new wav file back to the software – like Cubase or Pro Tools – and continue mixing! This is not a necessary or an important step but you can easily free some CPU resources this way, cause your pc/mac won't use the heavy midi programs but it will only use the new wav file you just exported, which is a lot lighter.

I will upload a separate tutorial that will show you how you can do this easily really soon.

14. Mixing Vocals – How To EQ Vocals, Compress Them And Use Effects

Welcome to my new **mixing vocals** guide. In this guide, I'll show you how to eq vocals, give you my personal vocal compression settings – techniques and in general, you'll see how to mix vocals and get them to sit in the mix properly.

Before I dive into advanced stuff and the plugin chains, allow me to say that you need some basic of knowledge of what compression, EQ and reverb is. If you googled your way here, then I suppose you know the basics.

If not, please click the following links to open new tabs to the following guides:

If you know what reverb, EQ and compression does, then skip the guides above.

If you don't, click the links to read them later, they're going to open in new tabs, so you won't lose what you're reading now.

Mixing Vocals – How To NOT Compress Vocals

In the chapters below, I'm going to show you how to mix vocals step by step, with images and videos.

But first, I'd like to have a little rant about some mis-information spread that confuses most people rather than helping them improve.

Note: *This rant was intended to solve many of your questions. It's not just a rant to fill in the gaps without providing any valuable info, I never type just for the sake of it. If you'd like to skip the rant please move to the next chapter. But I highly recommend you to read this chapter, it will help you a lot and shed some light.*

The most common answer I see people give to home recording newcomers to their question " *How can I get vocals to sit in the mix properly?"* is:

Record correctly, use some EQ and **Do not over-compress!**

While this answer is somewhat correct it's really not going to help. People in forums upload their new mix version with the "no too much compression" advice and 90% of the time the results are worse than before. But why is this happening?

I assume this is because around of 70% of the forum members in the internet, are consisted of hardcore old-schoolers, that grew up with led zeppelin, pink floyd, the doors, bands which I really love and admire. There's nothing wrong with that. Also these bands have lots of dynamics and again I love this fact, there's nothing wrong with dynamics.

The wrong part and my actual rant come to life when these old-schoolers give this kind of advice and never actually use it for themselves. But why am I saying this? They always say "trust your ears each mix is different, there's NO standard formula when mixing". I agree 100%.

But whenever the subject about dynamics comes up they ditch their own beliefs and suddenly the perfect answer for everything is DO NOT OVER-COMPRESS. No, please stop this people.

You cannot say that *each mix and genre must be treated different* **and on the contrary you say** *do not over-compress* **for everything**!

And that's pretty much what this rant is all about.

I understand that your old-school love for the old bands with dynamics has created a passion for dynamics, but either you like it or not the new modern genres actually sound better with more compression. I am not personally attacking you… It's just the way it is.

This is how people – including me – enjoy these genres either you like it or not, sorry.

When we listen to EDM or Metal we really don't care about dynamics, all we want is to listen to some in-your-face music! When we feel the need to listen to a genre with dynamics, we'll do.

Please stop acting like you're better if someone enjoys in-your-face music instead of your music choices with more dynamics. I think it's nice to have balance in your life and listen to music with and without dynamics, depending on your mood.

Modern bands, artists – DJs such as Nicky Romero, Evanescence, Linkin Park, Eminem and any other modern genre have less dynamics than we can imagine.

The artists just mentioned have got albums that are compressed a lot and it sounds really cool. So when people are asking advice about this kind of genres please stop saying "do not over-compress".

Or to say it better…

We should not apply old-school mixing techniques mainly created for specific old genres to new-modern mixes and genres. These ideas do not match. They just cannot co-operate.

Stop giving advice of how the producer from your favorite "The Doors" album mixed it, when someone wants to produce modern metal, hip-hop or EDM. Chances are that you're going to make that person's mixing life harder and his song will end up sounding like… you know.

Dynamics are nice, I love dynamics but to the right genre. Orchestral – Cinematic music needs dynamics for sure. Rock Ballads need dynamics. Chillout songs need dynamics.

But can you imagine *Machine's Head – The Blackening* (it's a metal album for those who don't know) with the "do not over-compress" mindset? I, for sure, don't want to imagine it.

Diving into forum threads and spreading the "do not compress much" rumor on EVERY SINGLE GENRE out there, even on genre that you DON'T LIKE is what really grinds my gears.

And in case you dislike modern productions (unfortunately I see lots of hate on forums) then please think before you give advice for something that you don't really know or like.

Isn't it logical and natural to actually give false advice for something that you hate…? It's simple logic really. This was *not* intended to insult an old-schooler.

This was intended to actually follow **your** rule that "each genre should be treated differently" which I agree wholeheartedly with it, and unfortunately, your old-school love for dynamics usually makes you forget to actually follow this rule that you *had firstly created*.

If you took this personally, please don't. If you do, maybe your gut is telling you to re-consider some things? If you got offended for something that is based on logic and wasn't intented for you, then I guess I might have a chance that I speak some sense here? If yes, let's try and stop the genre hate once and for all.

There's no reason for someone to be offended if he feels like he is not doing any of the above.

If you are really one of the group of people that don't any of the stuff mentioned above then you would have the "do people really do this kind of stuff" face. If you got angry or offended... I've got some bad news for you.

Compressing Vocals Properly

Since we should follow the "each genre is different" rule, there are certain questions you must ask to yourself in order to compress vocals properly.

Some of these questions are:

Do the vocals sound already compressed?

What's the genre I am mixing? Does it require dynamics or not?

Does the backing track – simply put the instruments – play at a steady volume? Or on the contrary, the instruments have lots of dynamics?

Get Vocals To Sit In The Mix

If you ask those questions then you'll start noticing something really important: **The vocal compression should be similar to the backing tracks.** That's how we should decide how compression we should add or not. But why am I telling this?

As I've talked in my compression tutorial, one of the primary aspects of compression is to bring the sound **upfront** with a steadier volume and less volume changes. So, depending on the genre we should apply similar compression.

In a hip-hop, EDM or metal song where the instruments have minimum dynamic range (meaning that the volume changes are almost zero) you can't expect to follow the "do not compress a lot" rule here. The reason is that most of the vocal phrases would disappear and hide behind the instruments.

As a result, we need to apply similar compression so all the vocal phrases can be heard. We can do this by either compressing a lot or automating the volume signal. I prefer using compressors most of the time.

You may now ask: *"But is it not dangerous to use lots of compression? Compressors act like crazy and it be heard in an unpleasant way"*. You're right but there's a way around this.

Should you decide to use compression, instead of automation, then read the chapter exactly below and you'll see a way of how you can compress a lot, without making it audible.

The Difference Between Compressing Too Much and Compressing Wrong

Let me distinguish these 2 terms, so I can help you compress better.

These 2 make newcomers to home-recording confused and they are afraid to use lots of compression, cause of all this nonsense spread that reducing the dynamic range of a song is necessarily bad, which is not.

Let's get this straight:

Compressing Too Much: This is simply compressing as much as you like, depending on your taste. It's wrong for some people, it's great for some others. It's not necessarily wrong or right as long as it sounds good to the right audience. Modern productions compress a lot. Old-schoolers prefer more dynamics. It's a matter of taste, neither can be considered wrong or right, cause it's purely based on taste and opinions.

Compressing Wrong: This happens no matter if you reduce the dynamic range a lot or not. This is not about opinions or taste. This can happen when you use the compressor in a wrong way that when a listener that has no clue about audio engineering can think "something is happening here and it's definitely sounding *not* cool". It's usually the sound of the compressors "choking" by abusing them in a wrong way.

The Solution: But how can we "abuse" the compressors and compress a lot – as long as the genre is asking for it and it sounds good – without making the compressors "choke"?

It's really simple. It's called: *Compressors In Series*.

Let's use an example to help you understand what *compressors in series* can do for your mixes:

Hypothetically, you've got an EDM song to mix. The producer used samples and kontakt libraries to produce the song so it's pretty normal for the sound to be already a bit of compressed. Then, he decided to use female vocals in his song.

He's hired a girl and started to record her wonderful vocals.

The instruments have already reduced dynamic range. The girl is not a sample obviously, so her dynamic range is way more broad. So we must match the vocal dynamics with that of the instruments… But he didn't use *some slight compression during tracking*, so he can help you mix later.

He simply didn't care, cause he might have thought that "you can fix it in the mix". So, you need to apply a bit more of compression to the girl's voice to reduce the dynamic range and match her vocals to the instrumentals. After some fine tuning your ears are telling you to compress at around -12db of Gain Reduction, which is **a lot**.

You fire-up your compressor and put the GR (Gain Reduction) at -12db. It sounds like @ ss. What to do? Simple.

You put the Gain Reduction back to -6db and you open a new instance of the same compressor (or different) and add 6 db more of Gain Reduction. The result? Same compression without the "choking artifacts" of the compressor. It's all about balance between these compressors.

The vocal phrases can be heard throughout the whole song and the listener is happy without thinking "what's happening here". Mission complete!

Important:

The 6db of Gain Reduction was just an example. You don't have to use the exact same amount of GR on both compressors. For example, you can easily use -3db on the 1st compressor and -7db on the 2nd. The are no rules here as long as it sounds good.

But how do we decide how much of GR we should use on each compressor? The answer is simple: It depends on what we want to achieve:

If we want to just shave the peaks with the 1st compressor without compressing the whole signal, we just tweak the threshold and listen. Was the sudden peak reduced and tamed, **without the compressor compressing the whole signal but just the peaks**? Good, move onto the next compressor.

What's the purpose of our 2nd compressor now that our peaks have been taken care off? **Gentle leveling**? Great! Since you want some gentle leveling, you can easily dig into the sound and you can allow the compressor to go deep compressing nonstop.

By nonstop I mean that the compressor is getting triggered **all the time**. The 1st compressor's purpose is to just "work" during the sudden peaks. The 2nd one must work continuously to deliver a constant volume throughout the singing.

Plus, it can do that easier with the help of the 1st compressor, cause it shaves the peaks.

So we're using compressors and plugins depending on what we want to achieve and we're not adding processors and effects just for the sake of it. That's how we should mix in general, not only during vocals.

My Vocal Plugin Chain

Now that we made some things clear about vocal compression and compression in general, it's time to continue this *mixing vocals* guide by showing you my usual vocal plugin chain.

Note: *As always, when I share my chains I advise you to bypass the plugins to actually hear if you're improving the sound or not. Sometimes, out of the 5-6 plugins I recommend, 3 or 4 might be enough for your mix. This entirely depends on how the vocals are sounding without any FX on it. I will share everything I use though, so you can experiment with everything and let your ears decide what to keep or not.*

Settings are random, the purpose of the added images was to help you have a vision of the GUI (Graphical User Interface) for those who don't know.

The Vocal "Warmer"

When we're working fully In-The-Box with zero analog gear it's wise to add a bit of analog "coloring" to the signal , by adding the necessary plugins.

A couple of plugins I really love for this issue, are the NLS plugin from Waves Audio and the Virtual Console Collectio plugin by Steven Slate (VCC).

Here are a couple of screenshots of both:

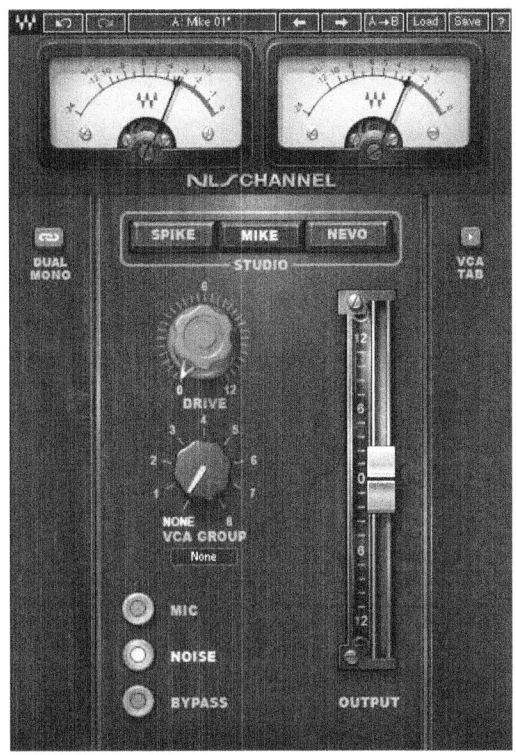

Chances are that you've recorded through an analog compressor and pre-amp combo that may have given you a warmer sound. If this is true, the sound you're going to get through this plugin might be "too much" for your liking.

It's a nice idea to try it out and let your ears decide if it must stay in the mix or leave. I've recorded through an analog amp and at the same time added VCC and the result was pretty awesome! So you never know if it's worth it or not until you hear it. Experiment!

Vocal EQ Tips

Next, I usually add an EQ to fix the problems or "bad" frequencies and enhance the "good" frequencies.

If you've got access to the *source* sound, being a microphone or a sample does not matter as long as you can tweak it, please go there to fix any problems, cause no EQ will make your track sound commercial if it was recorded/sampled like s**t.

EQ has the potential to improve your sound a lot, but it can't turn s**t into gold. But it can do the exact opposite if used improperly in an abused way. So please, if you can go back to the source and fix it there, *you'll save lots of time during mixing and the result will be a lot better*.

There are different kind of Equalizers, some with more knobs, some with less knobs, but in the end, all equalizers do the same and have the same purpose.

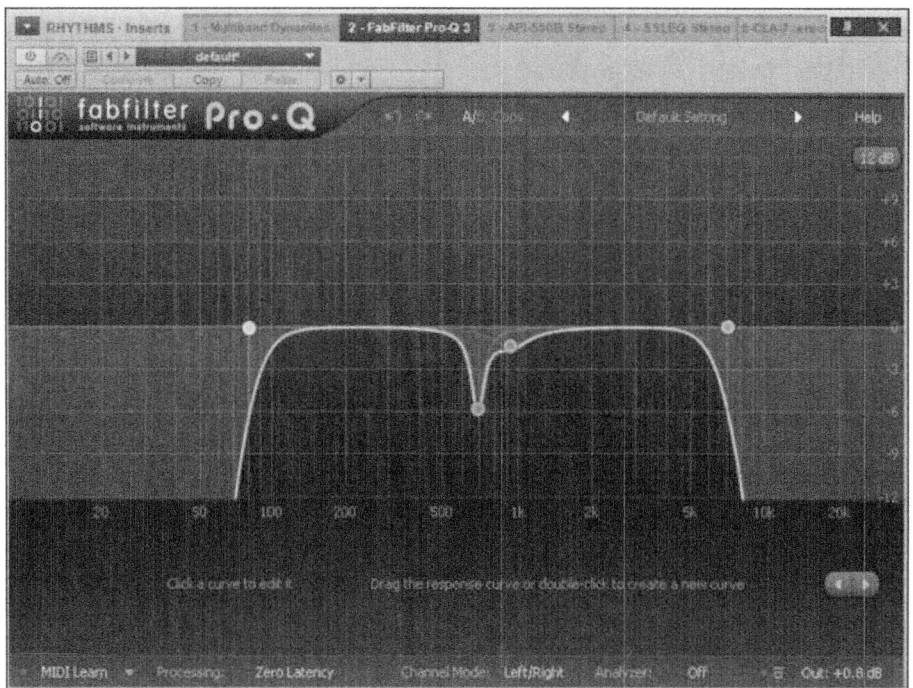

One of favorite EQs – Fabfilter Pro-Q

When you're EQing vocals make sure you try to do it while the whole mix is playing, so your ears can tell you when they cut through or get buried in the mix.

I usually solo them to reduce any annoying frequencies – resonances that won't deliver any useful to the mix and then I continue with the whole mix.

Here's a vocal frequency guide to assist you in your vocal mixing journey:

Fullness @120Hz Boominess @240Hz
Presence & Sibilance @5Khz Air @10Khz+
"Cut Through" Frequencies but also fatigue at around 3Khz.

Don't rely blindly on these. **Listen**. Chances are that you may need to leave the vocals as they are without any post- process.

If you've got vocal WAV files from commercial songs – some artists publish them – then it's wise to solo them and have a feeling of how far from commercial your vocals may sound, by using them as reference.

Vocal Compression Settings and Tips

Now that we've got some nice EQ going (or not depending on the source) it's time to use some compression to make our vocals and vocal phrases cut through.

I've explained how I use compression in general and especially in vocals on my rant section above – you can click it in case you scrolled your way down here. If you didn't read it, please do. It will answers lots of questions and clear some misconceptions.

Assuming that you've read the rant section I'm going to show you the plugins now. Let's begin.

This the CLA 76. This is mainly the compressor I am using to cut the peaks in an aggressive way so I can help the CLA-2A work easier below.

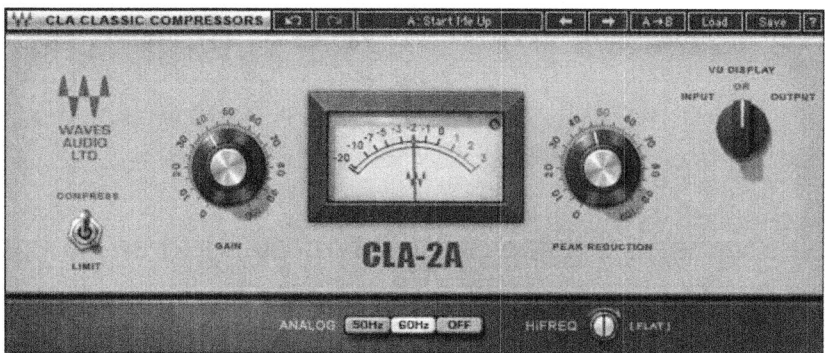

This is the CLA-2A. This compressor plays the role of making the audio sound more even across the perfomance. He's not so fast – and his job is not be fast – that he can easily be heard as being "choked" if some sudden peaks come through him.

That's the reason we're using an aggressive compressor that cuts the peaks right before so we can help these 2 co- operate.

I Don't Have These Compressors – What To Do?

If you don't own any of these plugins don't worry. There are 2 things you can do about it:

1. Just use a random compressor with a *fast attack – fast release* first in the chain to take care of the peaks and a compressor with *medium attack – medium/auto release* to play the role of the compressor that evens out the volume during the performance.

2. Check out the compressors guide. There are some *free* alternatives in there that can help you get the job done. I've also included download links.

Vocal De-essing Tips

Since we've compressed it's pretty logical for the annoying SS sounds to come to the surface. They are really annoying, hurt our ears and they must be reduced to avoid ear fatigue.

Every single DAW out there, in 2015, has a built-in vocal de-esser, unless the programmers gave up during their work and decided to ruin their reputation for trolling reasons.

Since the De-Esser is nothing more than a compressor that compresses/reduces the frequencies responsible for these annoying sounds, look for it at the *Compression*, *Restoration* or maybe even at the *Dynamics* folder of your DAW.

In case you want to know my de-esser of choice, please check out the video below. I show you my exact train of thoughts of mixing vocals from scratch, in a particular mixing session.

You may Subscribe Here**!**

As you can see I've added a couple of plugins not mentioned in this guide. Reason is that I rarely use them, I added them cause of this specific situation as I explain in the video.

I hope you've enjoyed this mixing vocals guide and hopefully I helped you clear up some things, so you can mix better sounding vocals.

And please don't forget: Each mix is different.

Let your ears make the final choice of what plugins to keep or ditch completely. If you've got any questions, you can visit our home recording community.

15. Monitors for Mixing and Mastering – Which should I choose?

Hello my friends, in this very first post I will give you some tips on how to choose the best monitors for mixing and mastering for your home recording studio.

Update: I have just created (7 – 15 – 2015) a post about the best studio headphones (opens on a new tab) perfectly written for people with really problematic rooms. Highly Recommended!

When you mix music you've got to be sure that you can listen to all of the frequencies with no distortion or alteration to the sound.

The most important thing for us is to own monitors that they don't give a unique "color" to the sound.

You shouldn't use your $50 Logitech speakers with the Realtek Audio Equalizer for mixing and mastering purposes. It might comprehend the sound when you're listening to music but when mixing we must aim for a sound as **flat** as possible.

You should give the freedom to your listeners to adjust the bass (or mids or highs) if they wish to do so, according to their preferences.

But your job is to create the sound and the **sound must be real**. If you use monitors with drastic built-in EQ settings then you'll end up with a fake "image" of the sound you're mixing/producing.

For example, you may hear more bass (because of the construction of your monitors) and when you're going to listen to your mp3 in your car, you will notice that there's no bass at all!

What needs to be done is that whatever you're hearing must be the actual sound and not a "fake" sound that your monitors create.

Monitors must be your friends and not your foes.

For this reason we choose *flat* sounding monitors that they don't color the sound.

High Budget Monitors

The reasons that I really loved the [Genelecs 8040a](#) are because of their honesty to my ears, the great bass they have for such a small woofer and the mids are also easy to be mixed.

I used to own these monitors and if you want to invest lots of money on monitors I highly suggest you to get these. In a couple of minutes, I will show you some fantastic monitors, cheaper that get the job done in this article below.

Update

I sold these monitors to get $290 ones. The difference in price was huge, but the difference in sound wasn't so great.

I've added an updated section below that talks about the new speakers, but let me explain a couple of things about monitors first.

What to look for in Monitors for Mixing and Mastering

No, you don't have to spend a fortune in order to create music.

Well if you have $3.000 to spend then do it, it's not my business hehe, but still you are not obliged to pay so much money for professional music productions, especially if you are just starting out. Just find a couple that you'll like – even if they are not "perfect" – spend some time with then and learn them.

That's the secret. To learn how your monitors are reacting. To master their "flaws". If you learn your monitor's sound by heart then you've just created a perfect audio system for your studio.

It doesn't matter if your speakers cost $3.000 or $300 as long as you know how they perform .

I know many people that mastered their $300 monitors and they never asked for an upgrade. Why spend money and time on something new, since they can mix perfectly using their… "old" and "cheap" monitors?

It's the human behind the hardware that makes the difference and not the actual hardware. Never forget this.

If someone is telling you that you can't have a professional sound without expensive monitors chances are that he is better at impressing people rathen than mixing professional sounding songs.

And, unfortunately, there are lots of these so called professionals that discourage new people to enter the "mixing world".

Why? Because they create the false reality to the new mixing engineers – you – that you need thousands of dollars to get started while you just need an $150 sound card, a couple of monitors, some programs and… passion.

Ok enough rant! Let me introduce you to some fantastic speakers my friends.

Monitors with a Perfect Price to Value Ratio

Price ranges differ and options are plenty. Many famous producers say that the Yamaha NS10 are the best monitors that ever made. They say that they have the flattest soundavailable and if the mix sounds good there, then it would sound good in every possible audio system.

It's pretty hard or even impossible to find these monitors because they are discontinued. But you can get their "children" as many producers call them the famous Yamaha HS80m or the Yamaha HS50m.

Their main difference is that the HS80m has an 8-inch cone while the HS50m has a 5-inch cone.

Bigger cone doesn't necessarily mean that it's always the best option though.

The 8-inch cone produces way more bass and most home studio owners don't own large rooms and they have no other option than placing the speakers right next to the wall.

The reflections of the wall boost the bass frequencies even more and you end up creating the first problem that I talked you about above – "faking" the sound!

So, if you are going to place the speakers in a small room without a proper acoustic treatment or next to the wall, I highly recommend to aim for speakers with a **4"** or **5" cone**.

There's no need buy 8" cones cause you'll end up with less money and poorer quality.

Let's not forget about the KRK Rokit 5. They have more bass than the yamahas, but still, I believe they 've got more bass than needed.

They **do** boost the lower frequencies so I recommend them for people that love genres heavily relied to bass (Hip Hop, RnB, Dubstep, Electro, etc).

Having said that, if you get used to this bass "flaw", their mids and highs really rock and they translate really well on every audio system.

The HS50m are better for small rooms and for rock/metal genres. They are also good for the genres mentioned above too, but some producers need in-depth bass monitoring for Hip-Hop (etc) so they also get a sub woofer along with the HS50m.

Neither Expensive Nor Cheap Solutions

If you don't have $3.000+ to spend for monitors but still, if you want to afford something better than the usual "low-end"
options – more than $500 less than $1.500 budget – then there are some really great options:

Adam A7X and Adam A5X : Both are really great monitors, more expensive though, but you will need less time to get used to them.

Mackie HR824: A medium budget solution for our hip-hop fans. Still a bit "bassy" but flatter than the KRK Rokits.

CRITICAL UPDATE – Winners in 2015

In the $300 price range, I would like to add the JBL LSR305 monitors.

Now that I've discovered these monitors I feel that they are the clear winners in this price range.

They are the ones that sound the most balanced between the KRKs and the Yamahas. Don't go for an 8 inch cone, though. Either get the 5" JBLs or the 8" Yamahas.

These are the best monitors for mixing and mastering out there, with the highest price to value ratio in the whole home recording world.

Conclusion

If you have the chance, I highly recommend to visit a music store and try them out.

Just get a favorite song of yours from a genre that you think you'll mix the most. Listen to this song to as many monitors as possible and get whatever "feels right".

If you can't visit a store and you are just starting out, try to get a monitor from the $300 range and start mixing. I'd get the JBL LSR 305 – Home Recording Pack with my eyes closed and won't look back.

Here are some songs I've mixed and mastered using the JBL speakers: My Work – Samples

Practice, practice and practice! It's the only way to get better. Good luck!

16. Reverb Tutorial – What Is Reverb In Music, What It Does, When We Need It And Its Controls

Welcome to our new reverb tutorial, we'll talk about everything reverb related in a really easy way to comprehend. This post has info for beginners but for advanced reverb users as well.

What Is Reverb In Music Production?

Many people wonder what reverb is, but in fact, we hear it every day! We even hear it right now.

All sounds before they reach our ears, even a simple conversation between your friends, hit some surfaces first (walls for example) and then we hear them.

Each surface gives a certain "color" to the sound signal *(we all sound better when we sing in the shower don't we? :D*

If We Could Give A Terminology For Reverb...

We create Reverberation when we send the sound to a closed space and "force" the sound to hit a surface and create a reflected sound that is heard again by its initial observer, known as **echo**.

*Hundreds of quick echoes produced together (with really tiny time differences in Milliseconds between each Echo) create the sound known as **Reverb**. Echoes fade away from time to time cause they are getting absorbed by the air and the surfaces.*

Why We Need Reverb

Every single sound that we can hear has Reverb in it (except the speakers that are **next to** our ears – the speaker of our cellphone for example).

We may not understand that we hear it, but it's there. It's a part of the sound that we got used to from the day we were born.

To Better Understand Reverb Let Me Give You An Example

Have you ever noticed how different the voice of a radio broadcaster is? It feels like it talks next to your ears. This happens cause there's no time for the sound to get reflected on a surface and create echoes. The sound is entering the broadcaster's microphone and gets redirected right to your ears!

As you can see, the lack of reverb may charm the broadcaster's voice but it's not the same for the vocalists or even for our whole mixes!

Without reverb, our mixes will sound weird on the vocals and some parts of the drum kit (snare and toms mainly). I will create a separate article with reverb tips but let's stick to the basic in this article

Controls and Parameters – Reverb Tutorial

Each Reverb plugin has almost the same knobs and settings.

But I will I teach you everything without leaving a parameter unexplained.

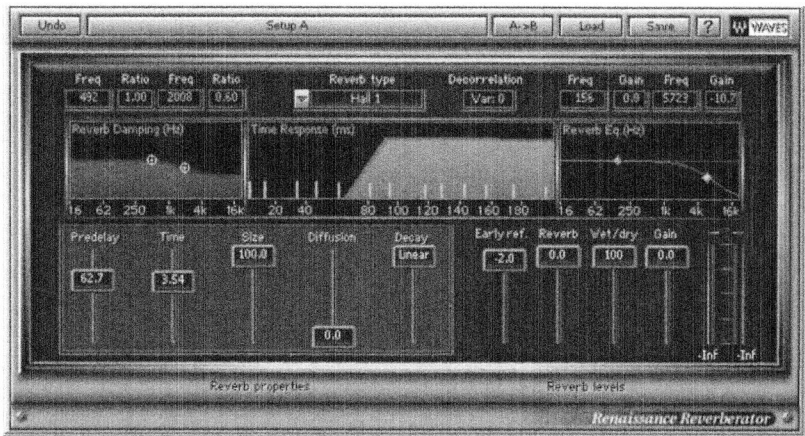

PreDelay – The time in Milliseconds (ms) that the sound needs to reach the wall (or any other surface). It's like moving the wall nearer or further-er from the sound. If the "dry" sound needs more time to reach the wall then we'll hear it more time without reverb. This is especially perfect for the vocals, cause we need to apply reverb to the vocals but at the same time we don't want to "drown" them with reverb. With no pre-delay at all we will possibly drown them resulting in vocals with no clarity. So, 40 to 100ms for vocals is a nice starting point.

Time/Decay/Tail – The time that the reverb needs in order to completely fade out or else the "tail" of the reverb. If the Reverb doesn't "glue" with the instrument/vocal and seems out of place chances are that you use too long decay.
0.5 to 3ms is a nice starting point.

Room Type/Size – How big or small the size of your room is. There's a difference between the sound and the size of a church and a small garage room.

Diffusion – How fast you "kill" the Early Reflections (read below).

Early Reflections – As the word implies, these are the very first reflections of the reverb before the original reverb. They give a certain "character" to the sound and at the same time they don't drown the sound in reverb keeping the sound's clarity in the mix.

Reverb EQ – If your reverb program doesn't give you EQ knobs then you can easily use your own EQ VST Plugin. This is perfect for cutting the low frequencies of the reverb producing "muddiness" in the mix and also cutting the annoying high frequencies that don't really flatter the reverb sound.

Damping – Similar to EQ but better for the higher frequencies. It's just a more natural way to reduce higher frequencies. You can think of Damping just like using… carpets and clothes to your digital room space, which in reality carpets absorb the higher frequencies naturally (damping) comparing to EQ which is considered to be an "external tool" to edit/reduce the higher frequencies. Both ways of editing are correct, there's no better or worse if the sound sounds good.

Reverb – Reverb. The slower Reflections after the Early Reflections that give a warm and sweet sound. Use this knob to blend the Reverb volume with the Early Reflections volume and vice versa.

Dry/Wet – How much Dry or Wet the final Reverb volume should be. It's the combination of both the Early Reflections and Reverb (slower reflections as I mentioned above).

Room Types

Now that we saw the Controls let's check out the room types.

Controls/knobs remain the same but the Settings change when you change a Room Type. Also each room type has its own characteristic sound.

For example, the sound is different when we sing in our bathroom and when we sing in the elevator… Let's check out the room types then!

Room

Oratorium, Austria

In the Room category belong the classic rooms that have a medium tail. (check out what tail means above). Some examples of Room Types are:
The WC, Professional Recording Studios that record their sound into software and you use it as a sample – known also as IR impulses (more about these in an another article) and of course any other types of rooms which considered to be small and medium sized.

Hall

Philips Hall (Small Auditorium), Netherlands

Halls are bigger rooms they are great to create an 80's sound to the Drums or the vocals.

The way they use it in the 80s though was so professional and I have no problem to listen to Depeche Mode and The Cure no matter that Reverb was really noticeable.

It's worth to mention that as time has been passing by reverb has been used less.

Today's productions have a really small amount of reverb comparing to the older productions. Especially in metal productions where you can hear reverb only to the vocals and the drums.

Plate

Plate Reverb

Plate Reverbs are artificial reverbs, they **aren't a simulation of a real room** .

That doesn't also mean that is bad cause it's one of the best reverbs that you can use on your snare drum. Using plate reverb on your snare, gives it a really fantastic sweet sound and the "tail" of each hit gives the sensation that the hit lasts longer.

As a metal fan, I really like to use more reverb in slower parts of a song.

For example, in breakdowns where the instruments pause suddenly and the reverb fades away, creates a "whoah!" feel, old but solid tip ^^

I was also amused with plate reverb on Vocals. Experiment!

Spring Reverb

Spring Reverb is the famous reverb type that most guitar amps have.

I don't really use it when I record guitars unless I feel like that I am not going to regret recording the sound this way. Just the fact that I don't like recording with spring reverb doesn't mean it's wrong though.
Everything is possible in mixing. You may even open a different VST by accident and create a superb effect (happened to me this month but with chorus not reverb hehe).

Clean Unwanted Frequencies Using EQ... Even On Reverb!

I always tell you how important it is to create room for instruments by cutting frequencies from other instruments that don't really need these frequencies.

Guess what then… I'll say this to you again!

You can't imagine how much frequency space the reverb uses. For this reason, it's a good idea to open an EQ (unless your reverb has a built-in one) and **cut till 500Hz** and **till 5.000hz** using filters – in short keep most of the mids.

This way you won't use reverb on the lower frequencies that that create muddiness in the mix and of course, you won't use reverb on the higher frequencies that get harsh when you apply reverb to them.

As you can see, mids play the biggest role when applying Reverb. And it's common sense to keep on EQ-ing if you like that just the high and low pass filters are not enough.

The biggest "secret" though is to find a reverb that sounds really good without any EQ on it and perfect with EQ on it.

How Much Reverb Should I Use? What Reverb Should I Choose?

Some common questions I come across are " **what's the best reverb** " and "**how much reverb should I use**"? I will be 100% honest with you just as I was when I started the blog…

If I won't listen to your mix, it's not possible to give you a correct answer and it would be not wise to answer in general… cause these questions can't be answered in a general way.

Each song, each track, each vocalist is a separate situation. It's like asking "what color should I choose for my car"?

But I Would Not Like To Leave You Disappointed, So Here Are Some Quick Tips That I Can Share With You:

* **Hi-pass and Low-pass filters** – Really help for the reasons I explained above.

* **Less is More** – It's true! Don't fall into temptation and think I CAN'T HEAR IT SO I NEED TO MAKE IT REALLY LOUDER cause you are just one step before overdoing it.

* **Mute** – If you feel like that the reverb can't be heard then try to Mute and check it out again.

* **A Happy Medium** – When you cannot distinguish Reverb while all the instruments play together but you can feel that something is missing when you mute it you are on the right track!

17. VST Instruments, VSTs and DAW Explanations

Today we'll talk about vst plugins, DAWs and vst instruments. These are really critical to our productions and it's the technology used by every famous producer of almost every genre out there.

DAW stands for Digital Audio Workstation

It's also known as Recording Program, Recording Software or Mixing Software. It is the program of your personal preference to record and mix music like **Cubase, Pro Tools** and **Ableton** to name a few.

Cubase is mostly used by European producers while Pro Tools is the No1 choice in the United States. Some other DAWs for you to consider are: **Reaper, Logic Pro and FL Studio**.

Reaper is a newer program in this field comparing to cubase and pro tools but it has frequent updates and promises a lot.

Many people switched to Reaper so I will create some videos for Reaper too.

VST stands for Virtual Studio Technology

DAWs work with VSTs. They are not standalone programs which means that they cannot be opened without using a DAW. In order to use VSTs you need a daw that supports them like Cubase.

VSTs are the **necessary** programs that help you mix. Programs like Equalizers, Compressors, Reverbs & Delays, Choruses and Limiters… every single processor and effect you are going to use is with one word… VST!

Pro Tools support RTAS instead of VST but it's the exact same thing, except the name. Finally, the Pro Tools company offers a more expensive version of RTAS known as TDM which they claim to have a better sound resolution that RTAS.

While you can hear an **insignificant** difference between these 2, I mostly believe that this is just marketing, so that the company can earn more money.

I've mixed the exact same tracks using VST, RTAS and TDM and the difference was really hard to notice. There are more important things that you should take care of for a great sound, rather than worrying about VST or RTAS.

VST Instruments

VST instruments are similar to vst plugins with the difference that these are not processors or effects. The little *i* next to *VST* stands for the word *instrument*.

Kontakt libraries and instrument libraries from a huge range of companies run in the VSTi format, which uses the VST technology to create an instrument – pianos, drums, violins, anything you can think of – instead of a mixing processor like compressors and EQs.

I hope you now understand the differences between VST, VSTi and DAW. Expect more articles from me for this subject! Take care!

18. What An Audio Interface Is Used For – Definition

Welcome to the **What Is An Audio Interface Used For – Definition** post.

Today I'll explain what an audio interface does, its main purposes and the reasons we can't use our default windows or mac audio card for music production purposes.

Let's start by giving a simple and non-technical definition of what an audio interface does.

Definition

Our audio interface is simply put our sound card.

It's the interface that's connected to our computers and transfer audio between your microphones and instruments. It's the also the gear used to playback, mix and master music.

While I have talked about the audio interfaces in the The Best 7 Value For Money Gear I've decided to create this separate post to keep everything nice and tidy.

What Is An Audio Interface Used For

An audio interface or sound card has multiple functions.

Apart from recording and mixing, it does some pretty neat things that we should not really care if we never plan to create our own sound cards, but it's nice to have a bit of an idea of what's going on behind the scenes. I'll keep it simple though without too much technical information.

There's a chance that some terms may be unknown to you, but worry not cause I got this solved.

If you're scratching your head about a word below, please click the link I manually put on each term.

You'll be redirected to a post that explains in simple words what each term means. All links will open to new tabs, so you won't lose what you're reading now.

Let's see the main functions of an audio interface:

Enables us recording by using either its inputs or MIDI data.
Converts the signal from digital to analog and vice-versa.
Enables you to push your CPU power as hard as you want by adjusting its buffer size.

Important factors to take into consideration, while choosing an audio interface:

Number of inputs and outputs. Number of microphone pre-amps. Stable drivers. *No ones wants his DAW to crash during mixing.* USB connectivity.
Low Latency.

In short, the audio interface is simply put the device that gives us the usability to record and mix music, by allowing us to connect analog instruments or even digital ones using VST instruments. Digital instruments run through your DAW.

We cannot use our default windows or mac sound card because:

It's got way too much latency and we won't be able to record.

Even if it didn't have latency, it lacks microphone and instrument inputs, so it's still pretty useless. Default drivers are not stable at all for music production purposes.

Printed in Dunstable, United Kingdom